10 THINGS

to Tell Your *Grandkids*
Because You Love Them So Much

NORTHWESTERN PUBLISHING HOUSE
Milwaukee, Wisconsin

D0584438

Cover and Interior Illustrations: Shutterstock
Interior Photos: James A. Aderman, iStock, Lightstock, Shutterstock, Unsplash
Art Director: Karen Knutson
Cover Art Designer: Megan Schable
Designer: Paula Clemons

Northwestern Publishing House
1250 N. 113th St., Milwaukee, WI 53226-3284
www.nph.net
© 2018 Northwestern Publishing House
Published 2018
Printed in the United States of America
ISBN 978-0-8100-2750-3
ISBN 978-0-8100-2751-0 (e-book)

21   22   23   24   25   26   27   10   9   8   7   6   5   4   3   2

Table of Contents

How This Book Came to Be 4

Having Conversations 5

1. I Pray for You 7–9

2. Thank God! 11–13

3. Go to School 15–17

4. Work Hard 19–21

5. Every Time I Look at You, I See Jesus! 23–25

6. Get to Know People 27–29

7. God Is in Control 31–33

8. If You're Going to Get Married, Marry Someone Who 35–37

9. God Keeps His Promises 39–41

10. I Know I'm Going to Heaven 43–45

Conclusion 46

How This Book Came to Be

What if a collection of inspirational articles could be gathered together and presented in a way that would touch on important spiritual topics that grandparents could be encouraged to discuss with their grandchildren? What if we could go a step further and include grandparents ahead of publication, asking them to read the articles, to actually have conversations about these spiritual topics, and to share their experiences with us to include in the book along with the articles?

That is how this book came to be. Not many of the grandparents who volunteered their time will say that it was easy. What I'm happy to report, though, is that they will all say they enjoyed their experiences, whether reading the articles, attempting fumbling conversations, or breezing through smooth little chats. They all were thankful for having participated and felt encouraged by the conversations they had with their grandchildren.

Have you ever seen the old trick where someone asks for a volunteer to step forward from a long line of people . . . and everyone except one poor soul steps backward? Similarly, most of these "Mentor Grandparents" were people I found out of the blue, asking for references through pastors all around the country. They had no idea this project was headed their way, had not necessarily viewed themselves as Mentor Grandparents before, and had no idea what they were getting themselves into! For their willingness to share candidly, I am thankful.

I ask everyone to remember that while enjoying their stories. This book will be a fabulous catalyst for internal dialog or group discussions about "What would I do?" in the different conversation scenarios. I only ask that you approach each story with Christian humility, imagining that these are grandparents that you have been introduced to after worshiping together and realizing that you share the desire of nurturing spiritual growth in your grandchildren. In fact, nothing would have made me happier than to gather all of these very different personalities together in the same room for a Bible class because, let me tell you, there would have been a lot of laughter, love of Jesus, and lively stories about the grandkids.

You'd fit right in.

Having Conversations

One day my middle daughter told me, "I can tell that you interview people for your job."

I'm pretty sure this wasn't entirely a compliment, since it was said in a characteristically toneless teenage way, but I still partly took it as one. I'm in the thick of the "I'll take anything I can get" parenting days, and I like to remain optimistic.

I understand that part of what she was trying to say in that moment, after I had just picked her up from her school activity, was that I have a way of trying to keep the conversation going, while others may be in the habit of simply exchanging a polite, obligatory greeting upon their child's entrance into the car. I was asking follow-up questions. I was "in my groove."

Alas, my studious, athletic, introverted girl had already poured her all into everything and everybody else for the day, and she was not interested in a conversation with her mom. But that was okay.

She started out answering a few basic how-was-your-day questions, but quickly hit her limit. When she expressed her clear indication that she was not interested in talking any further and I respectfully backed off, it allowed us to comfortably enjoy the drive home together, and we still built a bridge.

You may be chuckling at me, remembering moments like this that you experienced with your own kids or even that you may have with your grandkids now. If so, then you are more than prepared to have conversations not only about daily happenings but also about spiritual topics. How do I know this without actually knowing you? If you are identifying with this, I think I am safe in assuming that you understand (1) the basics of a two-way conversation, and (2) by simple nature of the grandparent-grandchild relationship and what God's Word says, it is part of a grandparent's job to pass scriptural knowledge on to the next generation. You can trust that God will not abandon you without the means and strength to accomplish the things that he has asked you to do.

Consider the words of King David in Psalm 78 as he clearly lays out the importance of each generation personally making sure the coming generations, children and grandchildren, know how wonderful the Lord is:

> My people, hear my teaching; listen to the words of my mouth. I will open my mouth with a parable; I will utter hidden things, things from of old—things we have heard and known, things our ancestors have told us. We will not hide them from their descendants; we will tell the next generation the praiseworthy deeds of the LORD, his power, and the wonders he has done. He decreed statutes for Jacob and established the law in Israel, which he commanded our ancestors to teach their children, so the next generation would know them, even the children yet to be born, *and they in turn would tell their children.* Then they would put their trust in God and would not forget his deeds but would keep his commands. (verses 1-7)

Continually educate yourself in God's Word, stay prayerful, and initiate important conversations with your youth. Ask them what they think, let them ask questions, and respect them when they prefer to table the conversations for later. As one of the grandparents you'll meet in these pages said, "You can't preach to them. You have to watch them and know how much they will accept. When they get on the defensive, you have to stop. There is a certain percent they have to learn for themselves. We have a long, strong relationship and they know my love is unconditional." Keep building your bridges, and they will know that they can keep coming back.

to Tell Your Grandkids

Included in grandparents' prayer lives is an additional category that was not there in our younger years—praying for our grandchildren.

Most of all, we pray that God would surround our grandchildren with knowledge of the overwhelming grace and mercy he demonstrated through giving his Son as the sacrifice that saves them from sin, death, and hell.

We pray that our grandchildren find the strength and comfort of sins forgiven, as they learn how to treasure the Word of God in their hearts.

And, of course, we can pray for all the topics in between sin and grace. Here are examples that have entered the lives of our grandchildren: Whether they are struggling with friends, can't decide if they should try volleyball or cross-country running, are wondering if they will ever

you get to talk with them about Jesus, *and* you give them a very natural way to include Jesus' name when talking with others. Telling someone else, "My grandpa called the other day and told me that he is praying for me," is a simple way for them to witness to their friends.

I called my grandchildren and asked them if they knew that Grandpa and Grandma prayed for them. Six of them realized that Grandpa and Grandma were praying for them. Three did not.

I also asked them if they thought about any special requests, knowing that they were on Grandpa and Grandma's prayer list. The three boys, all seven years old, had immediate ideas: pray for our whole family, thank you for praying for us, pray that my faith be strengthened, and help me believe in Jesus. The ten-year-old boy thought it was nice that his grandparents were praying

"As God's redeemed children, he loves to answer prayers for them—and you get to tell them that!"

have a first date, scraped a knee on the new Razor, got bit by a scorpion, found the pet chicken eaten by a fox, are getting ready for the first deer hunt, or just got yelled at by Dad, all can be taken to the Lord in prayer. "Do not be anxious about anything, but in every situation, by prayer and petition, with thanksgiving, present your requests to God" (Philippians 4:6).

With God's blessing, when we let our grandchildren know we are praying for all these different situations in their lives, the example we set will help them mature into Christians who don't put their trust in their own cleverness and abilities, but who truly take "every situation" to God in prayer.

You already include your grandchildren in your prayers, but do your grandchildren know that you are praying for them? Have you told them that Grandpa and Grandma consistently add them to their prayers? What impression might that leave with your grandchildren? You will enjoy the conversations that seem to erupt after you break through the awkward, initial silence. Yet most important, when you talk with them about prayer,

for him. He thought we should pray that he stay healthy. The 11-year-old boy couldn't think of anything to say. The 13-year-old boy felt reassured and very blessed that someone loves him that much. The girls (ages 10, 12, and 14) expressed their positive approval and thanked us that we were praying for them. One girl also liked the idea that now she could pray for someone who is praying for her. Besides these responses, they all had specific things going on in their lives for us to include in our prayers, as I mentioned above.

Now continued conversations and letters have a base from which to draw. It is a simple matter to ask about a topic that your grandchild had previously asked you to include in your prayers. Your grandchildren will also be reminded how special they are because, as God's redeemed children, he loves to answer prayers for them—and you get to tell them that!

This contact with my grandchildren was really worthwhile. I encourage you to remind your grandchildren just as Paul reminded the Romans, "Constantly I remember you in my prayers at all times" (Romans 1:9,10).

Matthew 7:7: "Ask and it will be given to you; seek and you will find; knock and the door will be opened to you."

Mentor Grandparents Respond

All of the grandparents involved in this project received this particular topic with enthusiasm. For people who believe in the power of prayer, it is easy to understand how meaningful it can be for grandchildren to find out

grandchildren's understanding of how you see them and their needs, no matter their stage of life.

~~~~~~~

Jawana H. is another grandparent who was willing to try this conversation with her grandchildren. She is 61 years old, lives in Milwaukee, Wisconsin, and sat down for this topic with her ten-year-old grandson and

"We pray for our grandchildren all the time but never thought about telling them."

that they are specifically being noticed and their concerns are being taken to God by their loving grandparents.

Sue P., Nebraska grandmother of 15, said, "I really liked this one. We pray for our grandchildren all the time but never thought about telling them. I asked our 22-year-old granddaughter, 'Do you realize that we pray for you?' She said she knew but hadn't thought about it much."

Sue also asked her granddaughter if she had any specific concerns that Sue and her husband could include in their prayers. By the end of the conversation, the granddaughter pleasantly surprised Sue by returning the sentiment, asking if she could pray for anything specific on behalf of her grandparents.

Sue had a follow-up question prepared, and I like that this second question didn't hinge on the success of her first question. What I mean is that if for some reason her grandchild had reacted unfavorably to the question "Do you realize that we pray for you?" and had answered in a disinterested or critical way, Sue could have still easily continued on just as she did. Lo and behold, the unexpected gem came out of the second question.

Another question that might be a great conversation starter is, "Do you want to know what I have been praying for you?" What grandchild can resist the curiosity of finding out what blessings Grandma or Grandpa has already been asking for on his or her behalf? If you should get that opportunity, it could deepen your

eight-year-old granddaughter. Are you ready to hear the results of this conversation? (Spoiler alert: it escalates quickly.) She said, "I asked them, 'Did you know I pray for you?' And they both said yes. So I asked, 'Is there anything in particular that you want me to pray for you about?' And they both said, 'To be baptized.'"

Jawana assured me that she was only left speechless on a very momentary basis before she talked to the children's mother to ask, "Did you know . . . ?!" She is prayerfully waiting now, hopeful for arrangements for the baptisms to be planned, and says she is thankful that because of this conversation, "I was able to be a part of this path."

It turned out that prayer was an easy topic of conversation for Jawana and these grandkids. After that spectacular start, she decided to ask them what kinds of things they were praying for. Answers varied from wanting other siblings to get a good education, wanting a specific toy, and being concerned for friends at school. It warmed Jawana's heart to hear how thoughtful and perceptive her grandkids were.

As for the most important thing about this experience, Jawana said, "It is ongoing now. Now we can continue the conversation. It's something we share."

~~~~~~~

_____

_____

_____

_____

_____

_____

_____

_____

_____

_____

_____

_____

_____

Moving Forward

You might want to make yourself an opportunity to share with your grandkids the important role that prayer has played in your faith life. An easy way to start this conversation is to simply ask about your grandchild's own prayer habits and offer practical examples of how you have fit prayer into your lifestyle.

If this is something you have personally struggled with in your lifetime, share your own earnest desire for a stronger prayer life and why it is important to you to make that change. Brainstorm together for specific ideas of how to fit more prayer into your days. How about agreeing that every time you see something special that reminds you of each other (when the moon comes up at night, when a new dandelion grows in the yard, etc.), you use it as a trigger to remind yourself to pause for a moment and ask God to bless your loved one?

When you are together, do you pray before your meals and at bedtime? If your family joins in these prayers, do you allow your grandchildren to make prayer requests?

If, over time, you start to notice that most of their prayer requests are for physical, earthly blessings, you can gently steer them to thinking about their spiritual, eternal needs too, as well as the spiritual needs of others in their lives.

Topic Two: Thank God!

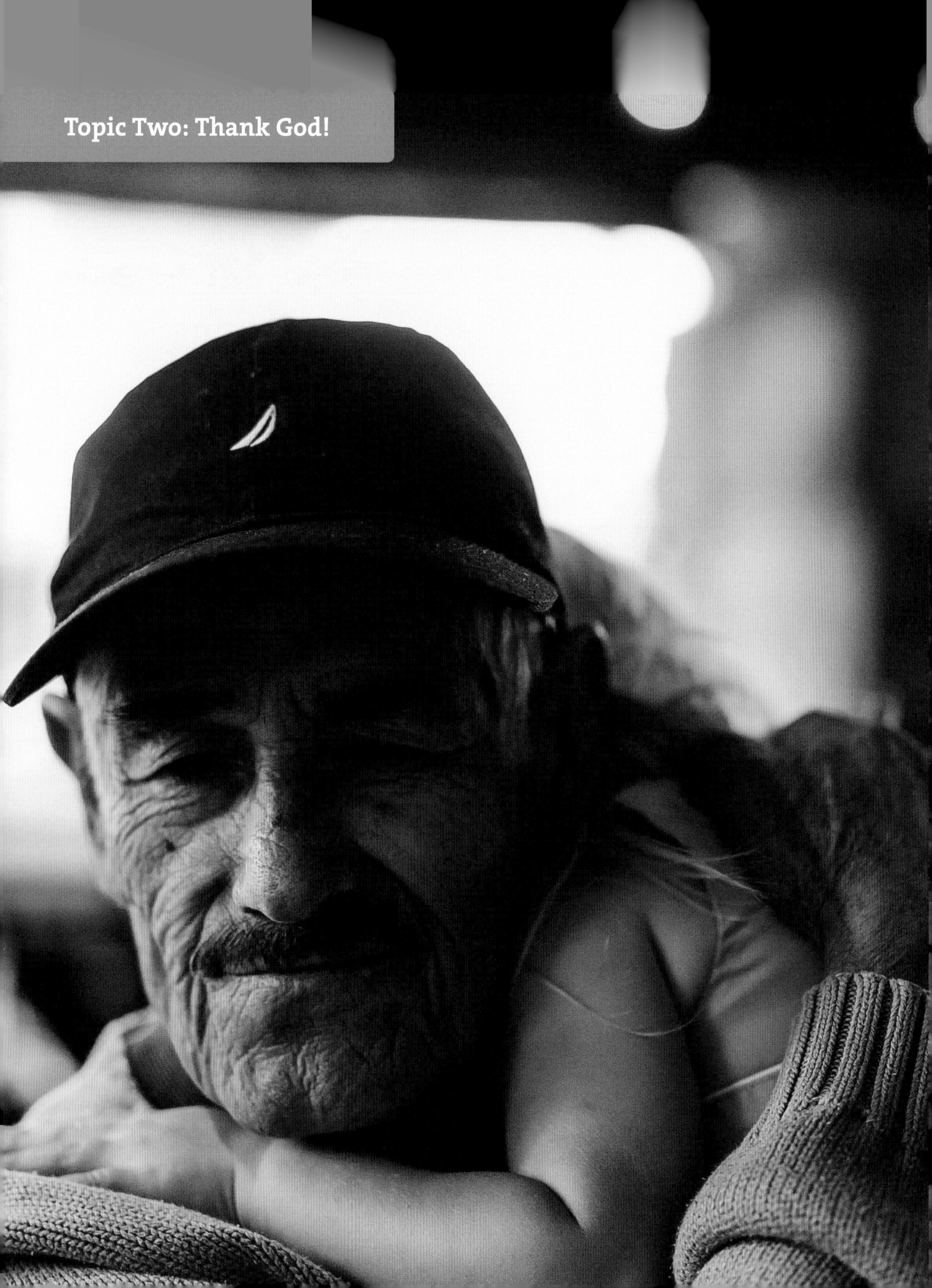

Grandkids hear plenty about saying thank you. Chances are, you have a lot to do with that. When they whine for something, you say, "I couldn't hear you. How do you ask me for something you want?" After the "please," we also instruct, "And now what do you say?" Whether they have just received a fruit snack or a gift for Christmas, we expect to hear, "Thank you!" Does God deserve less? Have you taught your family to thank God?

"I have! The grandkids come for a meal and we pray, 'O give thanks to the Lord, for he is good! His mercy endures forever!'

"And if that's not enough, we celebrate Thanksgiving every year: we worship at church; then at dinner we go around the table and everyone has to say one thing for which they are thankful."

This is a start, and we can all build on good beginnings. But thanksgiving to our Lord is more of a lifestyle than an occasion or a dinner prayer.

I often take for granted many of those blessings. How about you? How about your grandchildren?

What if they learned from Grandma and Grandpa to be thankful even for leftovers . . . the third time around? Even for hand-me-down clothes or thrift store bargains? Trips to the hardware store for the latest home repair?

Am I thankful for the loved ones and neighbors who make my house a home, or am I critical of them? Do the grandbabies see me thank God for the places in the yard that have too many weeds or for the health that still allows me to pull the weeds up? Do our grandkids hear us complain . . . about money woes, bitterness toward the company where we worked, our government, or the weather? That doesn't show an attitude of "Let's thank God!"

God intends thanksgiving to be worn like a new shirt every day. It is not dependent on how much we have or don't have. Thanksgiving is grounded in the knowledge that God, who owes us nothing, has generously given us

> ## "When you are with your grandkids, tell them how blessed you are to be with them."

One of my favorite lists of what to be thankful for was written by the great church reformer Martin Luther. The common people of his day had very little understanding of the Bible or of Christianity. So much of what Luther preached and wrote was to help them.

Every week, if not every day, they prayed a prayer first spoken by Jesus, and part of that prayer said, "Give us today our daily bread." Martin Luther tried to help the people to understand what they were praying for:

> Daily bread includes everything that we need for our bodily welfare, such as food and drink, clothing and shoes, house and home, land and cattle, money and goods, a godly spouse, godly children, godly workers, godly and faithful leaders, good government, good weather, peace and order, health, a good name, good friends, faithful neighbors, and the like.

whatever we have. It also recognizes that the Lord, who gave his perfect Son to die saving us, will also help us get through each day and will continue to bless us for Jesus' sake.

While the apostle Paul was imprisoned for his faith, things were meager. Yet he knew the secret to continual thankfulness: "I know what it is to be in need, and I know what it is to have plenty. I have learned the secret of being content in any and every situation, whether well fed or hungry, whether living in plenty or in want. I can do all this through him who gives me strength" (Philippians 4:12,13). (Check out the whole story in Philippians chapter 4.)

Thankfulness and contentment sleep in the same cradle, don't they?

When you are with your grandkids, tell them how blessed you are to be with them.

Smile more and thank God for the "old Ford." Give your spouse a big hug and tell the young ones that he or she is the best gift God gave you, second only to Jesus! And when you are praising our Lord in worship, with one grandchild hugging your arm and another squeezing your neck, let them see your happy tears. Tell them, "I am so blessed by God!"

That's THANKSGIVING!

Mentor Grandparents Respond

Leslie S. and her husband, Arnie, live in Georgia, and not so long ago their daughter's family lived in the same town and attended church with them. Most grandparents would agree that this sounds picture-perfect. Unfortunately, circumstances changed, their daughter's family moved to Texas, and many adjustments had to take place. Conversations that used to be in person are now mainly on the phone or face-to-face through the computer.

Leslie read the article and wanted to talk about the topic of being thankful. She introduced the conversation to her 7- and 11-year-old granddaughters by saying she had been reading to the students at their former school. (They know she remains an active volunteer there.) The book had been about Thanksgiving, so Leslie asked her granddaughters what they liked best about Thanksgiving.

Their answers included pie and family traditions of that sort, so Leslie prodded, "What does Jesus want us to be thankful for?" The girls were a bit shy about answering, so Leslie moved on and asked, "Can we be thankful when things are hard? Like when you had to move and we had to separate?"

At that question, Leslie could see each girl visibly reacting, seeming to get teary. She felt the need to recover the mood and promptly shared the very positive message of 1 Thessalonians 5:18, which says, "Give thanks in all circumstances; for this is God's will for you in Christ Jesus."

In reflection about the conversation, Leslie says she definitely would have preferred being together in the same room and doing an activity, such as baking, to help make the conversation feel more casual. As it was, it felt a little stiff. But for other grandparents who experience a less-than-perfect conversation, Leslie has important words of encouragement. "Keep working at it, like we do with anyone we want to share our faith with. Keep our eyes on the Lord so you don't get discouraged. Ultimately, it is the Holy Spirit's work, with or without us."

Does she think it will be less awkward the next time she attempts a conversation about a spiritual topic? She isn't sure. But interestingly, a couple of weeks later one of the granddaughters had a sports injury that resulted in a trip to the hospital. When Leslie spoke to her, she effortlessly and intentionally reinforced the previous conversation by using the words "I am so *thankful to God* that you are going to be alright."

~~~~~~~~~~

Jean K., grandmother of ten, was walking through the woods with her 7- and 15-year-old grandchildren and thinking about ways to have a conversation about thankfulness. She decided to ask them what it means to say thank you to somebody.

The seven-year-old admitted that sometimes a gift is so exciting that you forget to say thank you and need to be reminded. Eventually, the focus turned to who deserves the thanks and how to do that with prayer. Jean asked, "Why do we need to say thank you to God?" They answered, "Because he gave us his Son." "Jesus died for me."

"It was a ten-minute walk and an easy conversation that came naturally. We held hands and once and a while just gave a little squeeze," Jean described. "I did pray beforehand, 'Lord, make this opportunity happen. Help me say the right thing.'"

~~~~~~~~~~

Notes

_____

_____

_____

_____

_____

Moving Forward

What neat grandmothers we have in this chapter, sharing these uplifting conversations about thankfulness with their grandchildren. This immediately makes me feel thankful that there are grandparents willing to take the time to gently instruct.

Having an attitude of gratitude is in large part shaped by your vocabulary. I'm going to be so bold on this topic as to predict that the more often you find yourself using the words *thank you* in your everyday life, the easier it will be to find things to have conversations about that reflect a heart of thanksgiving.

When you are constantly acknowledging a feeling of appreciation toward others, many things will come to mind for which to be thankful. Not only that, but you will be generally known as a pleasant and kind person, and people will want to have conversations with you because they know those conversations will be uplifting and positive. That is a pretty cool side effect.

I never lived near my grandparents, so I can sympathize with Leslie. In college, I used to write letters to my grandmother detailing every mundane task I could think to write down, because I thought she might be lonely and would enjoy having mail in her mailbox. The intent was pure and the purpose was met, but the material was fairly meaningless. Since Leslie was picking up cues that face time was a little awkward in the first conversation, maybe she could turn to something more intimate like a written conversation with each girl. That could even give each sister some privacy. Some suggestions include old-fashioned snail mail, e-mail, texting, or even using something like a photo messaging app. If you were to exchange a "Gratitude Text of the Day," you would not only keep a positive attitude, but you would have a unique insight into your grandchild's daily life. Try, "Today I was thankful for . . . "

In Leslie's situation, I am so glad for her that she was ready for the opportunity God put in front of her during the second conversation she had with her granddaughter. Leslie didn't miss a beat; she was mindful about her intent to have a connection with her grandchildren about this topic in the long term. At her first opportunity to talk with her granddaughter to console her after her injury, Leslie chose her language carefully, to mimic their thankfulness conversation. Leslie told me she was certain the significance was not lost in the moment.

I hope for Leslie and her husband that there are many more opportunities for even deeper conversations about thankfulness in the future. After a health scare, or many other situations that come to mind, it isn't too much of a leap to ask to share a prayer of thanksgiving together. Leslie already bumped right up against this when she gave the glory to God by saying she was so thankful to him for protecting her granddaughter. Perhaps the next step in sharing a moment of gratitude could be listening to Grandma or Grandpa say, "Dear heavenly Father, we join together to thank you for this blessing."

Speaking of prayer, it is so important that our second grandparent, Jean, points out that she spent considerable time in prayer before attempting conversations with her grandchildren. In fact, it is clear that Jean's family is very comfortable being wrapped in prayer, and the entire description of her walk in the woods is enchanting in that regard.

I recall from the days when my own child, now a college freshman, was in preschool at a parochial school that the more often you openly discuss Bible verses and religious topics at home, the more comfortable and natural it becomes. I encourage you to make your time with your grandchildren a time when this sort of spiritual exploration is always allowed and in the open. Realize that you don't have to be an expert to foster this. If you don't know the answers to questions that come up, write them down and take them to church to ask your pastor.

Topic Three: Go to School

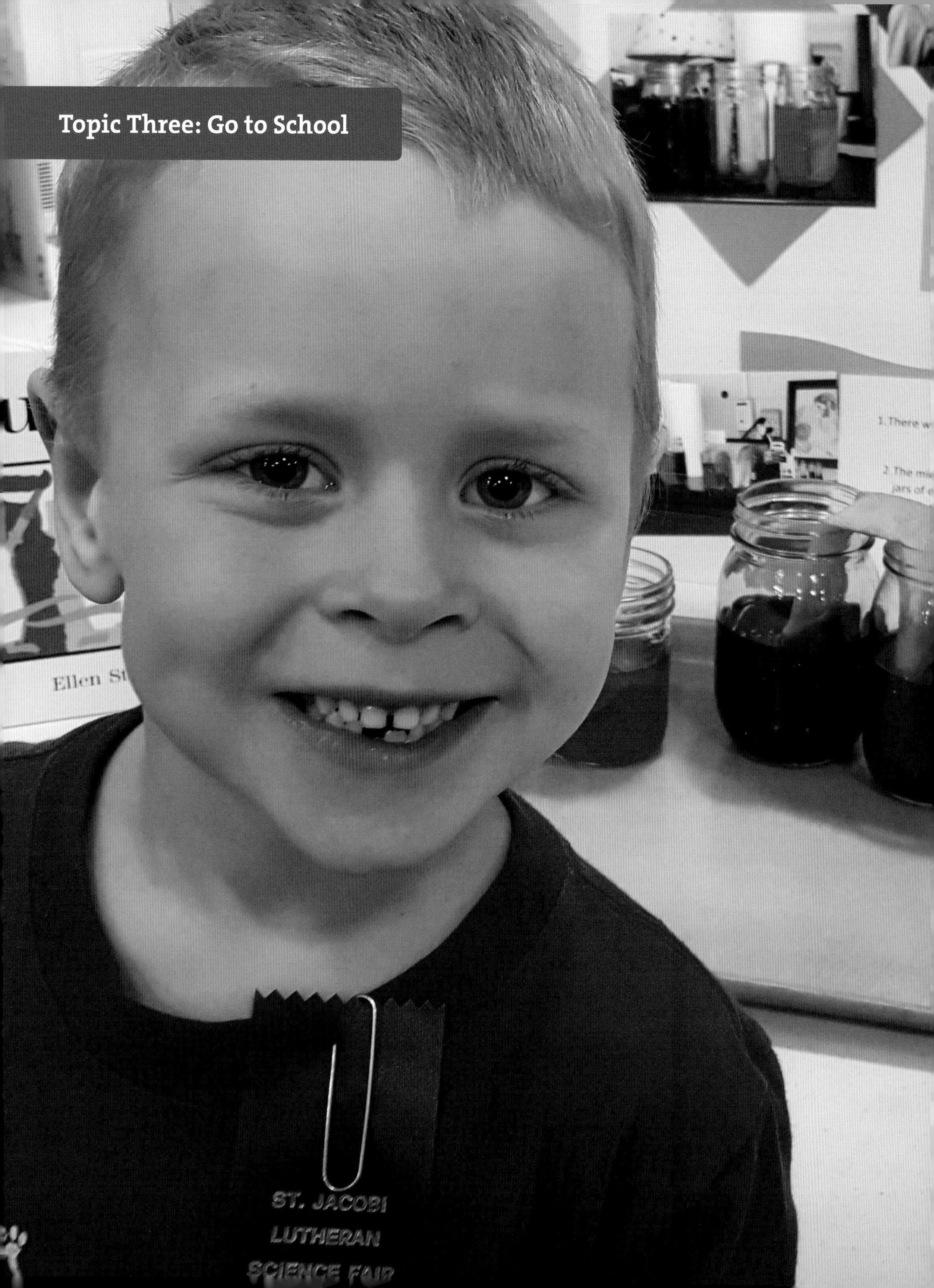

When I was in seventh or eighth grade, I was asked to teach a Sunday school class, filling in for one of the teachers. I still remember how wide-eyed those fourth graders were as I told them how God created the world in just six days.

Meanwhile, in my public grade school, science was one of my favorite classes. How could a 13-year-old not be excited about studying the mighty ferocious dinosaurs that roamed the earth millions of years ago?

I don't know when it happened, but somewhere along my educational path, *creation* and *millions of years* collided. Up until then, at least when I sat in my science classes, much of what I had been learning on Sunday mornings hardly crossed my mind. I'm glad I had someone at that point in my life who took the time to explain to me how Jesus wanted me to think about dinosaurs and science.

This was a turning point for me. This woke me up. Jesus is bigger than the Easter and Christmas stories. Jesus changes every bit of what I know and learn in school too!

time answering such questions at all. Or their answers might likely be all about worldly success: "So I can get into a good college." "So I can get a good job someday."

Consider the warning Saint Paul gives in Colossians 2:8: "See to it that no one takes you captive through hollow and deceptive philosophy, which depends on human tradition and the elemental spiritual forces of this world rather than on Christ." Paul also writes in 1 Corinthians 3:19,20, "The wisdom of this world is foolishness in God's sight. As it is written: 'He catches the wise in their craftiness'; and again, 'The Lord knows that the thoughts of the wise are futile.'" No matter what school your grandchildren go to, it may be easy for them to fall into the empty, worldly kind of thinking that says, "What really matters is how smart I can get," when what really matters is knowing and serving Jesus. It may be easy for them to start depending on their education instead of depending on Christ.

You have the privilege of reminding your grandchildren how all of their education has knowing and serving Jesus as the main purpose.

> "Jesus is bigger than the Easter and Christmas stories. Jesus changes every bit of what I know and learn in school too!"

Think how much time your grandchildren spend in school, plus doing their homework.

What if they need the same wake-up I needed? What if they aren't connecting their Jesus-learning with their school-learning?

It is natural to ask your school-aged grandchildren questions like, "How's school?" "What have you been doing in school lately?" and so on. It is natural to feel pride when your grandchildren are getting good grades, winning scholarships, or seem to have bright careers ahead of them.

But what if you ask your grandchildren, "Why is it important to know how to read?" "Why do good grades matter?" "Why are you learning a foreign language? Or biology? Or American history?" What kind of answers would you get? Whether your grandchildren go to a secular school or a Christian one, they may have a hard

Dinosaurs, the big bang, billions of years, and God's creation are common topics that most students will experience. Have you asked your grandkids what they think of all that?

But don't stop there.

You can remind your grandchildren how, to the mind touched by the light of God's Word, all school subjects reflect God's power, wisdom, mercy, and grace. History class shows God's hand controlling the events of the world as judgment day approaches. Music is used to sing the praises of our almighty God. Foreign language class provides new avenues to tell others about the love of Jesus. In science classes, everything studied, from leaves to nuclear physics, is an inspection of what God made. Physical education develops the unique body that God has created for each person. The list is endless.

Do you recognize the opportunity here?

Grandpa and Grandma, get your grandchildren thinking about how to use their education to serve Jesus. Help them "take captive every thought to make it obedient to Christ" (2 Corinthians 10:5). Guide them to love the Lord their God with all their mind (Mark 12:30), no matter what the teacher is writing on the board.

Mentor Grandparents Respond

Ron W. talks a mile a minute, tells a story like nobody's business, and is a self-described workaholic who celebrated his 60th birthday by going to work on a Sunday. He has four daughters and one son, but laughs because now God turned the tables and blessed him with seven grandsons . . . yes, all boys.

This article was a good fit for Ron because he values education so highly that he volunteers at the local elementary school. Ron drives a van in the morning for the small parochial school attached to his urban Milwaukee church. Daily, during the school year, he transports about 15 children to school. He says, "It allows me to mentor them, teach them to respect authority, answer their questions. I even had the opportunity to apply the law and gospel with a third grader who had spent some time in the office recently." (By "law and gospel" Ron is referring to God's two main Bible messages of judgment against sin [the law message] and forgiveness through Jesus Christ [the gospel message].)

Explaining that further, Ron said that in this instance he was given the opportunity to lovingly teach a young boy why it was important to accept the disciplinary process that he was experiencing at school. Ron often has contact with students who thirst for guidance from a strong male authority figure, and a lot of education seems to go on inside the commuter van, outside of actual school hours—education about navigating real life.

One thing he marvels at is the complexity of the questions they come up with, a feeling most grandparents can usually relate to. "Why is the sky blue?" "Why are some people called white?" "Why do they call me black?" Always searching for Christ-centered answers, Ron said, "I pray for God to give me the right things to tell them."

He also knows that taking time to provide answers, to educate, is another way to show children God's love. He says, "I still remember my first questions and who I could ask them to and who would take the time and not shoo me into a corner."

~~~~~~~~~

Becky K. is a 56-year-old grandmother of two. She teaches at a parochial school in a small midwestern city.

During her conversation, Becky's five-year-old granddaughter was in the backseat of the car while they were running errands. What a familiar setting for so many of today's busy families! It just goes to show that important conversations can fit into daily routines, which is one more way to keep God present in our everyday lives.

Becky asked her granddaughter if she loved preschool and what her favorite things were. Then they sounded out a couple of words and Becky said, "Pretty soon you'll learn to read. When you learn to read, what books do you think you'll learn to read?"

Becky was not expecting the answer she got. Her granddaughter thought for a moment and responded, "Maybe the Bible."

With such a big answer from such a little girl, Becky's mind was turning, trying to stay one step ahead.

"How will it help you?" she asked.

"Maybe when I have problems," was her answer.

Further probing resulted in a typical five-year-old's tangent that recapped creation and the flood, complete with the death of many animals. Becky felt like what had started as such a promising conversation, ended as disappointing as a big balloon that had lost its air. She had really hoped to lead her granddaughter to connect that by learning to read the Bible, she would be able to learn how to help *others*. But certainly, there will be other opportunities for more conversations, and clearly this five-year-old is very close to making that connection. It might only take one more talk with Grandma!

~~~~~~~~~

Jim A. is 67 years old. He and his wife have nine grandchildren, two residing in California and seven blessedly close to their home in a Milwaukee suburb. Jim is a retired minister who also holds a master's degree in journalism from Marquette University.

About a year ago, Jim started a Saturday morning writing club with his two oldest granddaughters. He and the two eight-year-olds named their club out of a creative combination of their initials. They typically find a Starbucks or other appropriate location for their work to take place. Jim knew this club was the perfect setting to approach a devotion conversation.

He decided to create a worksheet to go along with the topic, as well as an assignment, because that is usually how the club meetings work. He started out by saying, "I read a devotion this past week about why school is important. It made me wonder why you think school is important."

Then the three of them worked on their writing exercise, where the girls used a specialized worksheet to build their arguments about school being important, with the goal of eventually being able to write an article about the topic.

"If you don't get good grades, you don't pass," one granddaughter said. "You also learn from your mistakes . . . it forces you to try harder and to learn more," said the other.

Then Jim threw a new dimension into the mix and asked the girls to come up with reasons that were based on Jesus being the best motivation.

"Sometimes school is boring," said the first granddaughter.

"I understand that. I thought there were parts of school that were boring too. But let's talk about why doing well in school is important," he responded.

"Because in school we learn God's Word. [Jim's granddaughters both attend the same parochial school.] Is that a blessing?" she asked.

"Yes, it's a wonderful blessing," he responded.

"We also learn stuff in general. We learn about God's creation. In social studies we learn about other people and how they live," she continued.

The other granddaughter piped up and added, "The things we learn in school will help us when we grow up. Like math will help us pay our taxes."

The first granddaughter said, "You can also have fun in school. School isn't just about learning, learning, learning and stress, stress, stress. It's also fun, fun, fun."

Jim tied it all together with, "So you are saying that in school you learn to develop relationships with others; you learn how to be a friend. We should write that down."

After thorough conversation and full pages of notes, the girls left Starbucks with great material to write their articles about why it is important to go to school. I, for one, would enjoy being a fly on the wall to hear what these girls are capable of discussing with Grandpa at Starbucks when they come home to visit from college (or someplace amazing) in ten years.

Moving Forward

Have you ever felt unprepared for something? Being "properly educated" basically comes down to being properly prepared for life. Of course, this can look different for different people. What does it look like for a Christian, though? Are you a properly educated Christian? Thinking about your own education may help you have these conversations with your grandkids. How has your education been a blessing to you over the years as you have strived to serve Jesus and your neighbors? What opportunities to serve your Savior or share your faith would you have missed out on if your education had been less adequate? The answers to these questions could be great stories to start conversations with your grandkids.

Could your grandkids be running into contradictions like the devotion writer described from his childhood (millions of years vs. six-day creation)? What school subjects might include such contradictions nowadays, besides science and biology? You could ask, "Do you ever hear things in school that are different from what you hear in church or read in your Bible? Like what?"

Many kids love questions that get their imaginations going. You could try something like this: "If you could have Jesus himself for your school teacher each day, how do you think school would be different? How would it be the same?"

As your grandkids progress through their school years, their class subjects (and possibly the career plans they judge each subject's usefulness by) will keep changing. "What is your least favorite class? Jesus knew it would be your least favorite: why would he have you in that class now anyway—any ideas?" "What subject that you're studying now do you think will help you the most when you are a grown-up trying to spread the gospel and serve Jesus with your life?"

Topic Four: Work Hard

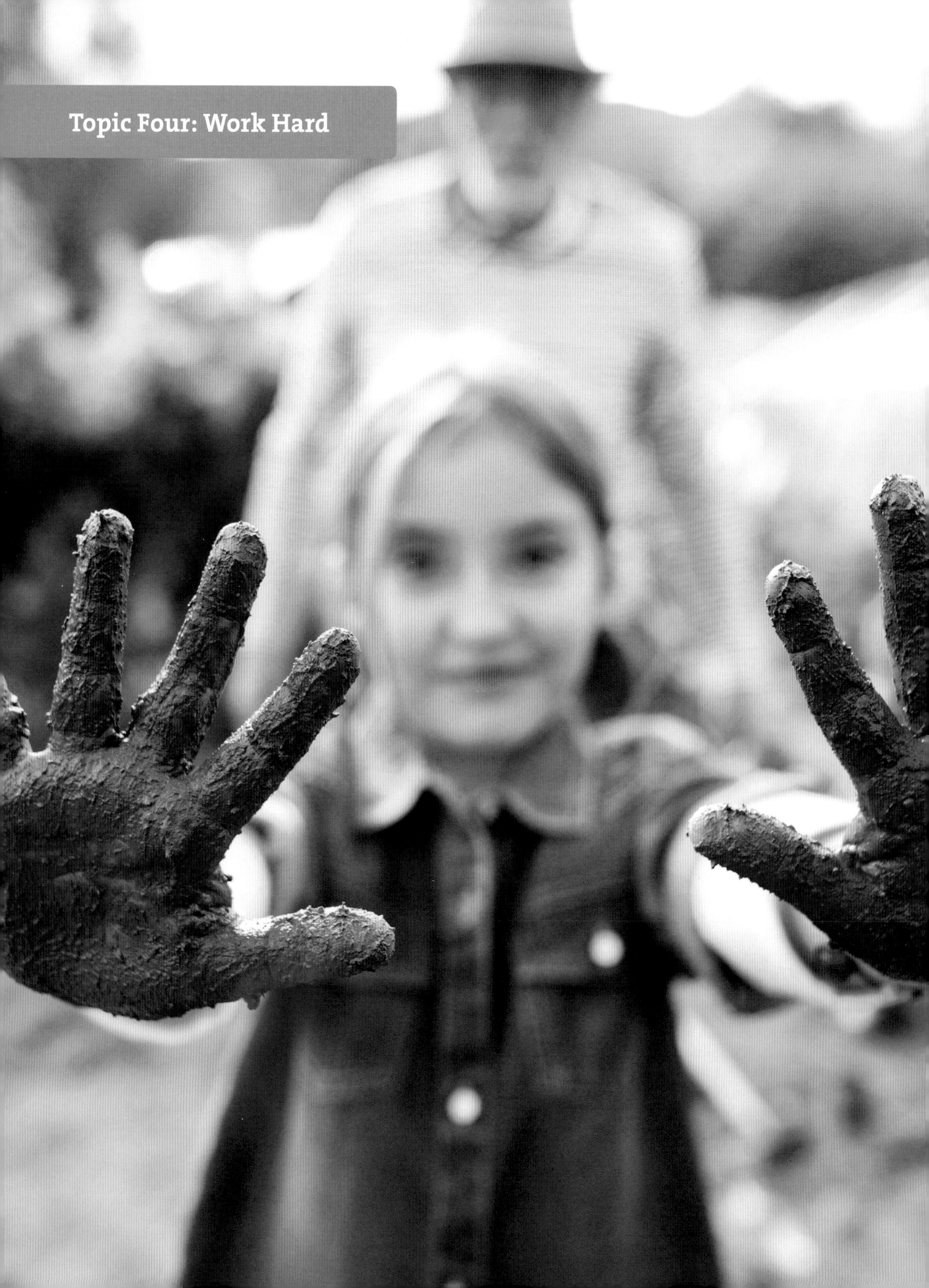

Betty went to her high school prom. She wore a beautiful dress, and her red hair looked gorgeous. Betty had a wonderful time with her respectful date.

The sun was coming up when she returned to the family farm. Her dad was walking out to the barn. He told her to go change clothes because she needed to help him milk the cows. Betty obediently changed her clothes and helped her dad milk the cows.

She was thinking that she could now go to bed for a few hours of sleep, but her dad had a different plan for her.

Betty is my mother.

Think back in your life. Who taught you the importance of hard work?

One of the main messages of the book of Proverbs in the Bible is to work hard. For example, Proverbs 10:4 says, "Lazy hands make for poverty, but diligent hands bring wealth." Or Proverbs 14:23 says, "All hard work brings a profit, but mere talk leads only to poverty." Or there's Proverbs 26:14: "As a door turns on its hinges, so a sluggard turns on his bed." Later in the Bible, the

"Who will teach your grandkids *why* Christians want to work hard?"

He told her that the bales of hay on the wagon needed to be stacked in the hayloft of the barn. Obediently, Betty unloaded the full wagon of bales and stacked them neatly in the hayloft.

She again thought that she could finally go to bed for a few hours of sleep, but her dad had more work for her to do. They went out to gather up the bales of hay out in the field and load them on the wagon. Betty worked all day long with her dad. Finally, after the cows were milked that evening, her dad told her to go into the house, get cleaned up for supper, and then she could go to bed. His reasoning for having her work all day, even though she was up all night, was to teach her that a person can have fun and enjoy events like the prom, but there were responsibilities that had to be met.

Betty never forgot what her father taught her that day. Less than a year later, her father died of cancer. While going to school, she milked the cows and took care of the farm.

That work ethic stayed with her all of her life. She became an X-ray technician at the age of 18 and retired at the age of 75. She passed that work ethic down to her children. She made her children get up early on a Saturday morning even if they got home late the night before. Today she volunteers at a medical clinic. Even though she is in her 80s, she has never stopped working.

apostle Paul often held himself up as an example of how Christians should work hard: "In all things I have shown you that by working hard . . . we must help the weak and remember the words of the Lord Jesus, how he himself said, 'It is more blessed to give than to receive'" (Acts 20:35 ESV).

Hard work isn't just wise and profitable. It is also a way to tell God we aren't taking him and his blessings for granted. And it is a big part of showing love toward others: "I will not expect others to work hard while I sit. I want to be of service to my neighbor!"

What parents wouldn't appreciate having help from the grandparents to teach their children that message? And to teach them *why* Christians want to work hard?

Perhaps you know someone like my mother—could you tell your grandkids that person's story? Or you could just ask them, "What does it mean to be dependable? Why is it bad for you to be lazy? Does Jesus want people to have jobs?"

Tell your grandchildren about the *blessings* of hard work.

Show them too. Let them see you working hard to serve others—in your family, at church, volunteering for those in need, etc. Find ways for them to serve *with* you. As you do, talk with them about why you work for others—how you know that your many blessings came to you from a gracious God "who gives you the ability to produce wealth" (Deuteronomy 8:18), and you want to show him you're grateful.

Mentor Grandparents Respond

Ron W. is grandfather to seven boys scattered over some challenging areas of the country for boys to grow up in:

and math. I said, 'You are not a C student. You're not fooling me.' He had no excuse. He said I was right." He was not applying himself, and he was being disrespectful to authority.

During that time together, Ron was able to share his philosophy about life and work and how that relates to kids. He explained, "For kids, it means school and upkeep at home and self-care. Your education: that's

> ## "This is what God expects of us: Anything we do . . . we sign our name as a child of God."

Virginia, Milwaukee, Detroit. He feels the full weight of every worldly battle vying for the hearts of his boys, telling them how fun and easy it is to throw caution to the wind and live for the moment.

Like many families, he is blessed to have some grandkids living nearby, while others are farther away. Many days, Ron's heart is concerned for his ten-year-old grandson almost eight hundred miles away, who is struggling in school.

This is not something Ron takes lightly. Truthfully, there isn't much Ron does take lightly. You must remember Ron from the last chapter, "Go to School."

Clearly, Ron is a natural conversationalist, and when trouble began brewing for his grandson, he developed a plan. Ron could see that it was time for Grandpa to offer his daughter—a single, professional mother—some respite.

Ron scheduled a vacation to spend seven days together at her house, five of which would be shadowing the grandson at school. There would be a lot of time for mentoring, teaching his grandson how to do chores around the house and yard, and there would be many opportunities for conversations. That isn't to say Ron is normally by any means a hands-off grandpa, but long-distance grandparenting does have its challenges. Compared to other visits this was going to have to be a more "grandpa intentional" experience.

Ron said, "I really worked with him and his teachers. He is a very smart kid, technically gifted with computers

what God would like you to be doing." The way he explained this to his grandson is as follows:

> I said to him, "This is what God expects of us: Anything we do . . . we sign our name as a child of God. God has given us the tools." That week, everything we did, from cooking dinner to cleaning our rooms, we did to the best of our ability. I'd ask him, "Did we sign our name to it?" There were some things we would look at and I would ask him to re-do, I think to his surprise. If ten people cut a lawn, you can tell which lawn I cut. I signed my name to it.

Ron and his grandson grew together and enjoyed each other's companionship that week. Now they are planning for his grandson to come to Grandpa's to spend half of next summer vacation for more bonding and to learn more about landscaping. I'm willing to bet Ron will come up with some other life skills to add to the list. Almost makes me want to take a road trip to Milwaukee so I can drive past Ron's church and see what landscaping project they "sign their name to."

On the far western side of Wisconsin live Carol and Jeff D., grandparents to nine adventurous cousins who do not live near one another but who gather for one week each August ("no injuries, no parents") for "Grandkid Camp." Living on ten acres of mostly wooded terrain, there is a lot of snake chasing, frog catching, designing and building with lumber scraps collected from the forest, and plenty of what Jeff categorizes as "out of the norm stuff" for the kids. Another element of Grandkid Camp is chores.

Carol explained that in the past, the older grandkids were expected to help in the kitchen. Last year, the littlest ones wanted to know why they were being left out. Moving forward, there will be a schedule and everybody will work together. Carol said she realized, "This is part of being a family. This is part of all being together."

~~~~~~~~~~

Notes

_____

_____

_____

_____

_____

_____

_____

_____

_____

Moving Forward

Hard work can look different for different people, based on ages and abilities. Do your grandkids have preconceived notions that younger people work harder than older people? Or perhaps, do you hold an opposite assumption? Have you ever dismissed somebody else's work because you are comparing it to your own? In reality, we know that no sweeping generalization about a large group is ever an accurate way to grow relationships. When it comes to hard work, all of us must always do the most that we can with what God has given us. Swap stories with your grandkids about the hardest jobs you've ever done.

But a big part of this discussion is *why* we work hard. Of course your biggest motivation is your thankfulness for Jesus dying to forgive your sins. How and when could you express that? Ron, Carol, and Jeff all made pretty extensive efforts to spend longer chunks of time side-by-side with their grandkids. Working hard on chores together gives a natural occasion for you to share your motivation for doing your best. "This is why I like to do my best at chores like this: _____. Do you ever feel or think that way?" you could ask.

Can you share a time when you knew without a doubt that God was using your efforts to bring him glory? Sometimes professional athletes and singers dedicate their performances to God. What would it look like if more people did that in regular life? Look around you and use your imagination.

Topic Five: Every Time I Look at You, I See Jesus!

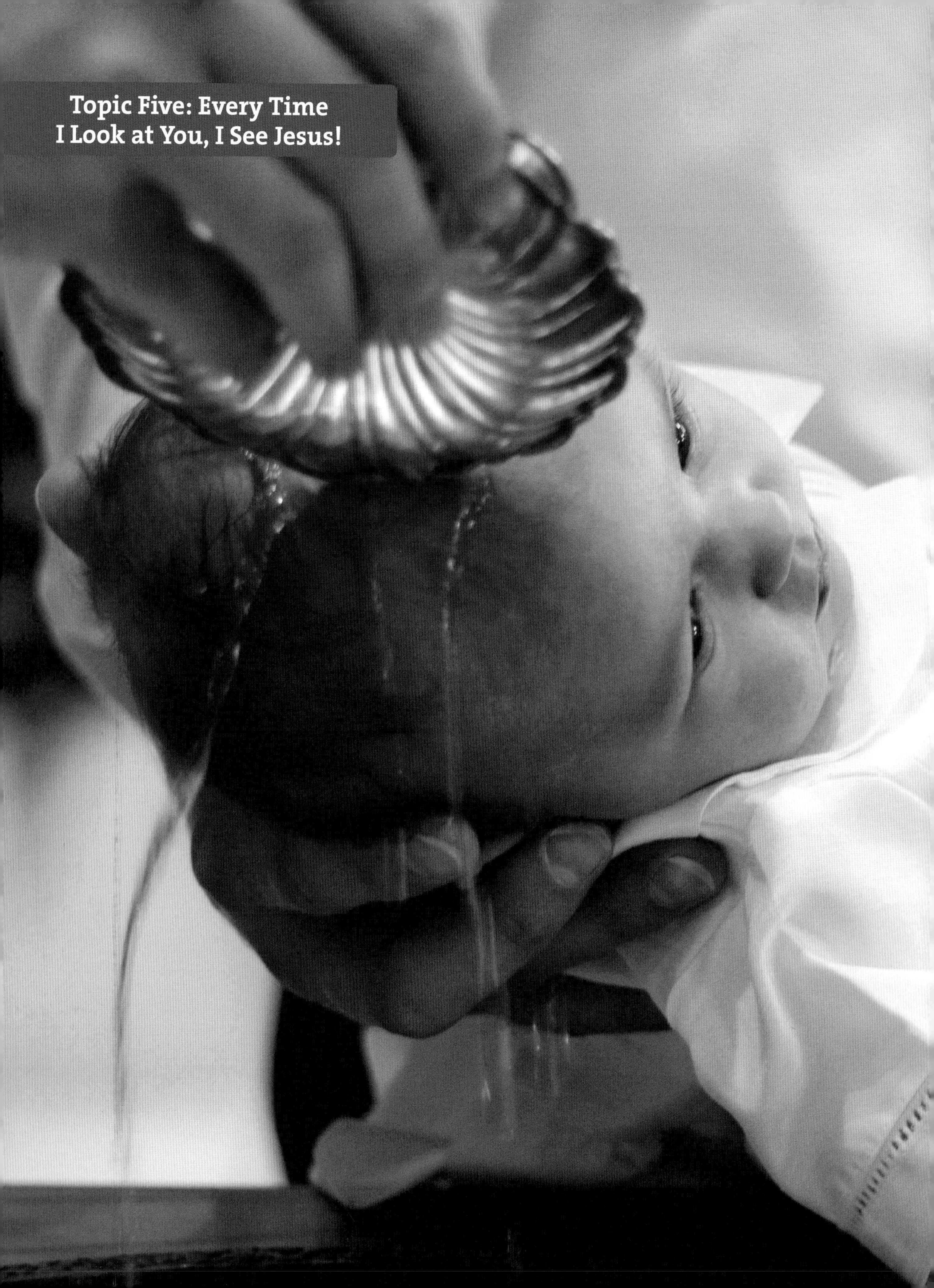

One of the happiest times for you and your grandchildren has to be their birthday celebrations. You mark them on the calendar, and if at all possible, you make sure you can be at the parties. Is there anything cooler than seeing the smiles on the children's faces as they open their gifts and struggle to raise their fingers to indicate how old they now are? Well, there is! It is their baptism.

I recently attended the birthday of a grandchild, and while at the house, I noticed a picture and banner from the grandchild's baptism. It occurred to me that while it was fun to celebrate the loved one's entrance into our family, how much more special it is that the loved one is a member of the family of believers through Baptism.

So in a quiet moment later on, I was able to say to my grandchild something I had heard a long time ago: "Every time I look at you, I see Jesus!" God has given us a reminder of Jesus on our face. You can explain to the child that our nose and our eyes form the image of the cross,

could say. You could talk about how you see Jesus in them now too.

I remember how my mom would knit little wall hangings marking the name of each grandchild and the date of his or her baptism. These were real keepsakes. But then cancer struck Mom at an early age, and on her deathbed she told me that she was ready to see Jesus, but she had two regrets. She explained that she didn't feel like she had ever brought someone to Jesus and, in addition, she would not be able to be at future grandchildren's baptisms. I appreciated her second regret, because being at the baptisms meant a great deal to her. But her first regret called for a response to her and for all of us.

Many times we do not realize just how much others can see our faith in the things we do and say. But God did use my mom. Through my mom, God brought my siblings and me to Baptism. God used my mom to raise us to be Christian, and we in turn brought our children

> **Many times we do not realize just how much others can see our faith in the things we do and say.**

and when you see the cross, you see Jesus and his love. "At your baptism you were made a child of Jesus through the washing of water and the Word of God. At your baptism you were marked with the sign of the cross on your head and your heart, marking you as a child of Jesus."

We might have other reasons for telling our grandchildren, "I see Jesus in you." We can point out the things they do and say that show their faith in Jesus. We can say, "Sometimes I think about how Jesus was your age once . . . " Or, "Some of my happiest memories are the times I have come to your church to see you sing." But it can all come back to that day they were "clothed . . . with Christ" at their baptisms (Galatians 3:27).

Of course, if people grow up not thinking much about their baptism, they will miss out on a lot (if not all) of baptism's power, won't they?

What a privilege it is, then, for us grandparents to speak to our grandchildren about not only their baptisms but the baptisms of the grandchildren's moms and dads and aunts and uncles—our children—and the blessings God gives through Baptism. "Did I ever tell you about the day your Daddy (or Mommy, etc.) was baptized?" you

to Jesus in Baptism. Our children are now bringing the grandchildren to Jesus in the same way.

None of us know when the Lord will call us home to heaven. Perhaps many of us will not make it to all the baptisms of grandchildren. However, as long as God gives us the opportunities to celebrate their earthly birthdays, why not use that occasion—and many others—to speak about and to celebrate with them the gift of Holy Baptism, their birth into God's family!

Mentor Grandparents Respond

When you sit down for a heart-to-heart with a four-year-old, you just can't predict what you're going to get. When you ask, "Do you know what Baptism means?" and the innocent-eyed child tells you it has to do with grown-ups going to the grocery store . . . well, you know that child was trying really hard to please you by coming up with the "right" answer.

Lisa and Sam C., of Georgia, are in their early 50s and relatively new to grandparenting, but they were up for the challenge of having a conversation about Baptism with their grandson. They were nervous and felt awkward, which might be a common stumbling block. They started where we all should start when we're nervous, with our most powerful, yet most overlooked, tool: prayer.

After Lisa and Sam found spiritual guidance and had a brief discussion with each other, they sat down with their grandson and started to talk. Because of his initial confusion about the definition, what transpired ended up being a lesson on what Baptism is:

> I told Aiden that when he was a little baby, Pastor came to our house and picked him up and sprinkled water on his head and said a prayer to God. I also told him that when Pastor was finished with the prayer and the water, this meant that he is now a child of God and Jesus is now with him all of the time. Aiden said, "Is he in my tummy?" and Sam said, "Yes, but Jesus is also in your heart."

> Sam said to Aiden, "Aiden, you know when you take a bath and you get really clean? When you are baptized, the water is like Jesus' blood and it washes away your sins." Aiden looked pretty puzzled by my husband's statement. My husband told him that sin is the bad things that people do.

At the end of her explanation, Lisa said,

> I then asked, "Do you love Jesus?" and he shook his head yes. I then stated, "Me and your grandfather love Jesus too." My husband at that time reiterated to Aiden that Jesus is now in his heart because he was baptized. Sam also asked him if he liked Baptism and he said, "It is really good." We all three gave each other high-fives and we told him that Jesus loves him.

> In reflection, he was very quiet and receptive. He seemed to be truly listening. I don't know if he really understood Baptism literally, due to our delivery. But I believe the Lord was sitting on the couch with us and he touched us.

~~~~~~~~

Barb C., a 51-year-old grandmother of two, read the article about Baptism and scheduled a lunch date with her two granddaughters, whom her son has joint custody of. They are one- and five-years-old, so she anticipated the conversation really being with just the older granddaughter.

Barb started by asking the five-year-old if she could help her talk about Jesus (don't little ones love to be helpers?) and talk about her little sister's baptism. Barb said, "She remembered that she and the baby had pretty dresses on, and she said it gave her goose bumps . . . and I thought, *WOW—that is DEEP* . . . but then I realized she meant she thought the water was chilly!"

Moving along, Barb reminded her that at the baptism they all prayed that Jesus would watch over her baby sister and then took the conversation in the direction of prayer, because she knew that was an area her granddaughter was more familiar with. They continued talking about that and their favorite Bible lessons while they lunched.

While it may seem like this baptism conversation didn't work, I'd say Barb's first attempt went well and she has a lot to build on next time. It is very exciting to establish that her five-year-old granddaughter has such a vivid memory of the baptism, and it will be fun to revisit that another time.

Sometimes a question goes over like a lead balloon, and there is just nothing you can do about it. Do what Barb did—move on. If a grandchild doesn't have an answer for you or doesn't understand your question or you seem to be talking past each other, don't let it become a distraction that derails your conversation. Isn't it wonderful that Barb was able to swiftly shift gears over to a different topic that she knew her granddaughter would have something to comment on?

Becky K. is a 56-year-old mother of two and grandmother of two, ages 2 and 5. She and her husband are blessed to live in the same small city as their grandchildren and are very involved in their grandchildren's lives.

After reading the article about Baptism, Becky, snuggled together on the couch with her granddaughter, pointed out to her that it was going to be her birthday the next day. She asked if she knew what other special thing happened on her birthday. Her granddaughter did not remember, so Becky told her that she had been baptized on her birthday and asked her if she knew what Baptism is. Her granddaughter needed a description, and Becky concluded by saying that Baptism made her a child of God. Her grandchild proudly responded, "I know I am!"

The conversation continued as her granddaughter became very interested in asking about other people she knew and whether or not they had been baptized. Had her mommy been baptized? Had Nana? She also wanted to know where different people had been baptized, since some had been in churches, yet her baptism had been in the hospital shortly after her birth. Becky reinforced, "We want everyone to be a child of Jesus."

Trying out the wording from the article at one point, Becky said, "When I look at you, I see Jesus." "Oh, Nana, you're crazy! I don't look like Jesus!" her granddaughter giggled.

Enjoying the lighthearted exchange, Becky showed her granddaughter what it looks like when a pastor baptizes and blesses, making the sign of a cross over the head and the heart. Becky asked her, "What does this look like?"

"A cross!" she identified immediately.

"And who does the cross remind us of?" Becky asked.

"Jesus!" came the answer.

Becky also asked her, "Can you see Jesus in me?" and got an interesting answer in response.

"You don't look like Jesus." Her granddaughter reflected. "You act like a Christian. You teach children about Jesus, you are nice to people, and you pray with me."

Becky has always used a certain catch phrase with her students at a Christian school, and it seems her granddaughter has heard and learned the meaning of it as well: "If your behavior doesn't make Jesus smile, you shouldn't be doing it."

~~~~~~~~~~

Notes

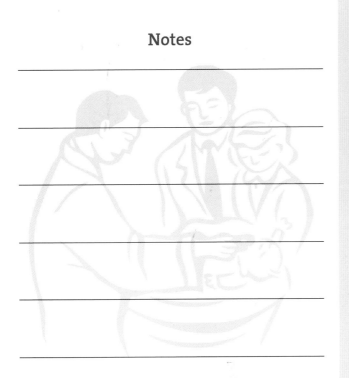

_____

_____

_____

_____

_____

_____

Moving Forward

Several of these grandparents may have walked away from their conversations feeling doubtful that the objective had been met. The truth is, there are endless results that can be considered successful when initiating conversations with grandchildren! If you feel like the topic is a little daunting, seek guidance ahead of time, like Sam and Lisa did, through prayer and with the leader of your church. Be aware that kids are unpredictable, and be willing to move with the topic in whichever direction your grandchild takes it. You will have to adjust your expectations depending upon the child's age and maturity. It is okay to decide to return to the topic on another day, like Barb did. Grandchildren are still learning to be comfortable with the conversational experience, which is also part of the equation.

Many families used to track baptisms by writing the dates inside the family Bible. Does your family own such an heirloom? Is there a modern day equivalent, or how do today's families make personal records of special events? What does this say about the place for religious traditions in today's culture?

When is the last time you reflected on the significance of your own baptism, rather than thinking about or planning for someone else's baptism? Spend some time sharing old photographs of family baptisms (including your own!) with your grandchild.

And remember, as wonderful as the event of Baptism is, this topic of seeing Jesus in your grandchildren isn't just about what happened years ago with water and the Word. If you don't get to spend much time around them yourself, ask their mom and dad how the grandkids have been acting like their servant-hearted, loving Savior lately and then let them know how happy such reports make you.

You are concerned about who might be friends with your grandchildren. I feel the same about mine. It is important they not fall in with the wrong kids. This is a good topic for conversation with them, but it can be tricky. You want them to evaluate their relationships, not judge them yourself.

Maybe you could get at it this way, to help them sort out good company from bad. Talk about friends you have had in your lifetime. There are the people who were good to know, and there are those the apostle Paul warns about when he says in 1 Corinthians 15:33, "Do not be misled: 'Bad company corrupts good character.'" Were you ever misled by bad company? You might find a way to talk about that without ruining the good image your

asked me how I could be so calm. I could honestly tell her it was because I trusted Jesus to keep his promises to take care of me. She wanted to know more. In these situations I was not trying to be a pastor to someone. I was simply living the faith the Holy Spirit has given me. We can encourage our grandchildren to do the same.

But if living out our faith can make an impression on strangers, how about on friends?

Friends are people who have learned from experience that when they're having problems, we'll be good listeners. Maybe our grandkids need to be encouraged, "One of the best things you can do is to be there for people, as a good Christian friend. Get to know them.

"Jesus wants us to get to know people, especially those who need to know him."

grandchild has of you. If you can, it could be a big help to that child. Of course, it is easy to talk about the good folks you have known who have influenced you to walk the right paths.

Our grandkids may need the warning, "Watch out who is influencing you." But perhaps what they need even more is the encouragement, "Get to know people: be a Christian influence."

Christian children can easily get the impression that all unbelievers are "bad company" and must be avoided. No, we must not avoid all unbelievers. Our Lord Jesus told us to "make disciples of all nations" (Matthew 28:19). He wants us to get to know people, especially those who need to know him. In my own experience, the more I got to know unbelievers, the more I saw that most of them are nice people. Many were kind and respectful, responsible and trustworthy. They were not people I needed to avoid. They were lost souls who needed Jesus.

It is true that complete strangers can see Jesus in us sometimes. I could tell my grandkids about the time a stranger in a fast-food restaurant made a nice comment about seeing me pray. Or about the time I was on an airplane that was trying to get around a big storm. The lady in the next seat became very uneasy with all the bouncing around as the winds buffeted the big jet. She

Let them see you up close and learn what it means to be a believer in Christ."

This also answers a concern we may have when our grandchildren go off to college or to their first job away from home or into the military. Will their life with Jesus survive? If they know how to live their faith and keep it strong, then when they make friends, their friends will notice. I learned this from a young lady in our congregation who went off to Army boot camp. Before she left, she asked me for a copy of a devotional magazine our church gave away called *Meditations*. Two weeks later she called and said she needed more of them. She had been sharing her copy with girls she had met, and they wanted to have their own to read. Her faith didn't just survive, it spread.

Lord Jesus, help us to get to know people so we can share with them the good news about you as Savior. Amen.

Mentor Grandparents Respond

Mark G. is a grandfather of 13, and after living quite literally all around the world (at one time Mark was a missionary), he and his wife are now blessed to be living in a small midwestern city near many of them. After reading the "Get to Know People" article, Mark looked for an opportunity to talk with his eight-year-old grandson about the idea of being friends with kids who are not Christians.

This was not an unfamiliar concept for his grandson, because his grandson had accumulated some rather big experiences for being only eight years old. He had moved from one state to another, he had attended both public and parochial schools, and he had made a wide variety of friends.

Mark simply needed to ask him what he thought about it and give him a chance to talk. His grandson had a lot of ideas, including the mind-bending treasure that follows: "Whenever two or more of us gather in his [God's] name, he is with us. So if we are sharing our faith with someone, he is with us, so we really aren't alone with our friend. There are three of us. So we don't have to feel nervous or afraid." (Following the mind of an eight-year-old boy can be exhausting!)

Mark found that his conversation unearthed many treasures and wanted to share his grandson's insight regarding our motivation for nurturing our Christian friendships. "Sometimes I'm weak in my faith and I need help from my Christian friends, and sometimes they're the ones who are weak and only a Christian friend can give the help that is needed."

~~~~~~~~

Carmen G. raised four daughters and now has eight grandchildren and one great-grandchild. She and her husband have been married for 41 years. When Carmen's children were young, she and her husband sent them to a parochial grade school. When the girls reached ninth grade, they transitioned into a public high school. Carmen recalls, "It was a big shocker for them. We were called in because one daughter was teaching the Bible and debating other religions in the lunchroom," she chuckled.

After reading the "Get to Know People" devotion and remembering this story about her daughter, Carmen shared the memory with her grandchildren. At first the story sounded shocking, but then they were not terribly surprised when they found out which aunt it was, based on her passionate personality. Then an honest teenage comment surfaced, giving the aunt a lot of credit: "I wouldn't have argued with that person. Everybody would be looking."

~~~~~~~~

Moving Forward

The different reactions of Mark's grandson and Carmen's teenage grandchild help us see that kids have widely ranging comfort levels when it comes to the idea of talking to their friends about their Savior.

Where are your grandchildren on that wide-ranging spectrum? If someone starts asking them questions about their faith, would they be able to provide solid answers? Can they back up their answers with Scripture? Even if they can, perhaps there are some faith-building Bible passages that you and your grandchildren can commit to memory together. If you are unsure of which ones to start with, many of the passages used in the inspirational articles in this book would be good. Or check with your pastor for passages that make good answers to the questions that your grandkids' friends are asking them.

"Everybody would be looking" was an honest comment, but also the kind of comment worth following up on. These are the follow-up questions I wish I could ask Carmen's teenage grandchild, but unfortunately in the writing of this book it wasn't possible to travel to all the grandparents' houses and meet all of their families: "Where is your comfort level? You don't have to have the same approach as your aunt. She liked debate. Great for her. If that sounds far too intimidating, I appreciate your raw honesty. Now, what is your alternate plan? What will you do instead? How will you help strengthen someone's faith? How will you spread God's Word?"

I do love Carmen's story. First, I picture it like a movie scene in my mind, with Carmen's teenage daughter eloquently winning an impassioned verbal battle against her peers. Second, I think it is great that Carmen told a story to the grandkids about their aunt, bridging the gap among the generations. Kids crave those kinds of stories. And if there are hidden stories of spiritual heroism waiting to inspire the kids in your family, ask yourself, Why aren't you sharing those stories? What are you waiting for?

Surely this was an inspirational story for Carmen's grandchildren, and I'm not entirely convinced that they would never debate their faith like their aunt. If my imaginary questions to Carmen's grandchildren seem a little pushy, it is because I've talked to Carmen and heard her story firsthand and I've heard her describe her grandchildren, and let me tell you, there is some spunk in her family's genes! I would be shocked if they had a problem standing up for what they believe in.

Teenagers (especially) like to be dismissive in their responses. "Oh, I'd never . . ." Don't let them underestimate the ways their Savior can use them to make other people into his disciples. Instead, push through and call them on it. Try a compliment that keeps the conversation on track. "But you are very confident and well-spoken! You were on your eighth grade debate team!" or "That's funny, I thought you helped teach Sunday school this year, and I bet you answered a lot of questions!"

You may want to encourage your grandkids to get to know people so they can share their faith. That starts with getting to know your grandkids, their faith, and what they think about sharing it.

Topic Seven: God Is in Control

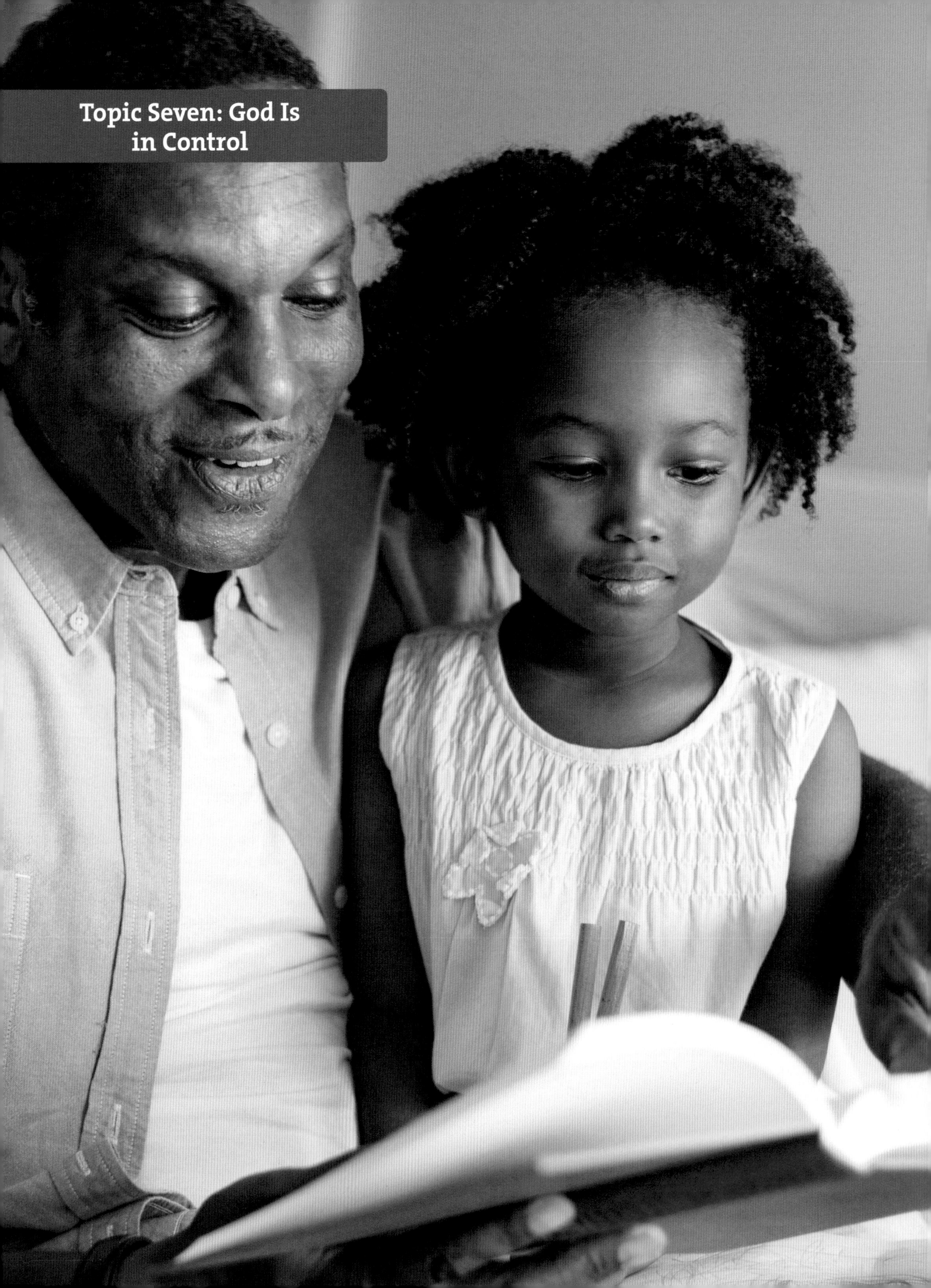

"The world is sure going to h*** in a handbasket!" Can you remember Grandma and Grandpa speaking such words? Then they would elaborate: "I sure wouldn't want to be your age" or "I sure wouldn't want to be growing up in a world like this." I remember my grandma, my great-aunt, and others talking to me that way.

Now maybe I shouldn't, but I have gotten old enough to think and talk that same way. You may have different things that scare you about the world nowadays. But here are some of mine. When the news on TV talks about Christians being beheaded in the Middle East, I'm afraid for what's coming. Human life in general, especially of those who cannot speak up for themselves, seems to have so little value. Nobody can just plain get along anymore: everyone is so argumentative. And

Your perspective of what's wrong with the world can be helpful to your grandkids. It can serve as an antidote to the anti-biblical views of the culture around them.

Grandkids need to know, when they run into the corruption of the world around them, "This is the stuff Grandma and Grandpa warned me about. This is what they pray I would stay out of. This is not Christian." Won't that be a source of strength?

But it's important not to be hopeless about the future.

You can do more than say to your little ones, "Here's what I'm afraid the world is going to do to you."

You can say, "My grandma was afraid too when she looked at the world I was growing up in. But I survived."

"Now you can look back on your life and see: your grandparents' prayers worked."

what's happening with climate change? Every time I pick up the newspaper, I get depressed.

Should you share those fears with your grandkids, once they are old enough?

"I'm glad I'm not your age" might not be the best conversation starter. But your grandkids are probably hearing about many of the same news stories and moral debates that you are. Why not just ask, "What do you think about _____?" Find out what they're hearing in school and from their friends and what they think. Maybe they have the same fears as you. Maybe it hasn't even crossed their minds that there's something to be afraid of. These are good conversations to have.

Some of the biggest names in the Bible—Moses, Jesus, Paul, John, etc.—especially toward the end of their preaching ministries, made a point of letting the next generations know, "The world is just going to worse." These very godly men (including our Savior) said clearly that the future would be bleak, that trouble and evil times were coming. These men, under the Holy Spirit's guidance, saw the wisdom in warning the younger generation of the great dangers that the worldly culture around them would be bringing their way.

Yes, not only have you survived; you still, after all these years, have your faith and trust in the Lord.

How encouraging it would be to have a conversation that ends up like that!

What did your grandparents do with their fears of what was coming of the world? They took those fears to Jesus in prayer. And now you can look back on your life and see: those prayers worked—yes, you fell into temptations, you fell for some of the world's lies, but in the end your grandparents' Savior is your Savior too and is more than able to keep you safe. He is bigger than the world and all its depressing evil. He is in control. Isn't that a great perspective to share with your grandchildren?

Jesus didn't just tell his disciples what the world was becoming and what it all would do to them. He said, "In this world you will have trouble." But then he went on to say, "But take heart! I have overcome the world" (John 16:33). He lives, risen from the dead, and all authority in heaven and on earth has been given to him (Matthew 28:18).

Take comfort, fellow grandparents, that God is in control. Look back on your lives, on how he protected you in the world that so frightened your grandparents. Encourage your grandchildren with that same comforting protection.

Mentor Grandparents Respond

Karen and Jeff B. (both age 63) raised seven children and now have 16 grandchildren (and counting!) spanning five different states. When the family is gathered and the adults have conversations that touch on spiritual topics, they try to also include the children. Jeff is a pastor and Karen is a teacher, and perhaps because of this dynamic, they find that this happens regularly.

For example, almost immediately after reading the article reminding them of God's constant control over everything, Karen and Jeff found themselves gathered in the kitchen with two of their daughters and sons-in-law discussing the presidential election, while the grandchildren worked on a craft project at the table.

There were five children present, the oldest being an eight-year-old. Karen asked her if they had been talking about the election in school, and she said yes. Karen and Jeff made sure to include her in the conversation about the election and which leaders were in charge. They asked her, "But who is *really* in control of everything?"

It warmed their hearts as she had no hesitation in her answer: "God is in charge!"

When Barb C., who also participated in the conversation for "Every Time I Look at You, I See Jesus," contemplated how to discuss the topic "God Is in Control" with her five-year-old granddaughter, she wasn't sure at first what the best approach would be. A social worker by profession, she considered what things her granddaughter might feel were *out* of her control and therefore scary.

Barb was scheduled to have her granddaughters at her house for a sleepover on a night when storms were in the forecast. This seemed to be a fitting circumstance, as nature is certainly out of human control and entirely within God's domain. Barb set out to have a conversation with her granddaughter, where the child quickly volunteered, "I'm scared of thunder and lightning."

Barb told me, "I brought in prayer and talking to Jesus when we are afraid. She said she was also excited about school starting but afraid there might be bullies there. Again I said, 'When you are scared, what are some things that you can do?'"

"You can talk to Jesus," she answered.

"I really enjoyed the exercise," Barb said. She explained that she had gotten immersed in the adult world over the years and had lost touch with the simple joys a conversation with a preschooler can bring. "The neat thing is, you are in the mind-set with your own kids, but you kind of forget when you aren't around it all the time with your grandkids. Having done the exercise, I know I can. It was pretty easy."

You most certainly can think of a personal story to share to emphasize the peace God puts in our hearts when we trust in him. Harold B. is a 91-year-old great-grandfather from Tennessee with priceless stories to share with his grandkids about more things than we can fit in this book. One interesting facet of his life includes his military service as a young man. He described, "When I was overseas for war, I remember praying and saying, 'Do I want to be a hero or be assigned to something less dangerous?' But I didn't fear it. Now I can talk about all the things God brought me through . . . the ways the Lord was blessing me. In the end, I got sick and couldn't leave with the crew. That saved my life."

"Recently, my oldest grandchild just happened to call, and I took the opportunity to retell my story. He thanked me for sharing that and reminded me of another story I had," chuckled Harold.

As Harold told it to his grandchild, the miraculous story deserves repeating here. In 1913, before he was born, his young mother took a desperate journey by oxcart with two young children across the Ukraine to the North Sea through battlefields and minefields, arriving in time for, as legend would have it, the last boat out, navigating torpedo infested waters and eventually finding way to Ellis Island to reunite with her husband who had taken previous passage.

Harold quickly credits, "If you don't think God is intervening . . . even the fact I'm here is a miracle! It happens in everyone's life. Do you realize that your being here and my being here is a product of what God did? Somehow God knew this . . . that my descendants would do his work. I was supposed to be here to get those kids going. You're here for a reason. And I guess that was mine. I'll be talking with more grandchildren to get it into a conversation."

In other words, God is in control. Tell your stories and teach your grandchildren to find peace in these words, or the world will tell them not to.

Notes

_____

_____

_____

_____

_____

_____

_____

_____

_____

_____

_____

_____

_____

_____

Moving Forward

Are you a person who sees the glass as half full or half empty? Do you find comfort in the idea that God is in control, or do you feel contempt? Most believers are comforted by the idea of God having "the whole world in his hands," because it means that we don't have to carry the weight of the world's problems on our shoulders. There can be times, though, when even faithful people get caught up in overplanning, only to see things not come together the way they thought they should. The worldly reaction can be downright skeptical: "If your God is in control, why does he let bad things happen?" Where do you fit in? Being honest with yourself about your own fears for the future is key here—then you can share with your grandkids your own fears (in an age-appropriate way) and share with them how you plan to hand those fears over to your Lord.

If your fears about the future are too grown-up to bring up just yet, talk with your grandchildren about a time in your past when things were outwardly out of your control but God showed the power of his mighty hand.

There are many biblical examples of chaotic moments when God rose up and took command. Find some of these passages and refresh your memory together with your grandchildren. One suggestion to start with might be in Exodus chapter 14, when the people of Israel left Pharaoh's captivity in Egypt. As Pharaoh chased after them, God parted the Red Sea for their safe passage. Or try the account in Mark 4:35-41, where Jesus and some disciples were caught up in an unexpected squall on the Sea of Galilee. Rather than capsizing and drowning, as the terrified men surely thought they might, Jesus simply calmed the storm with his words.

Topic Eight: If You're Going to Get Married, Marry Someone Who . . .

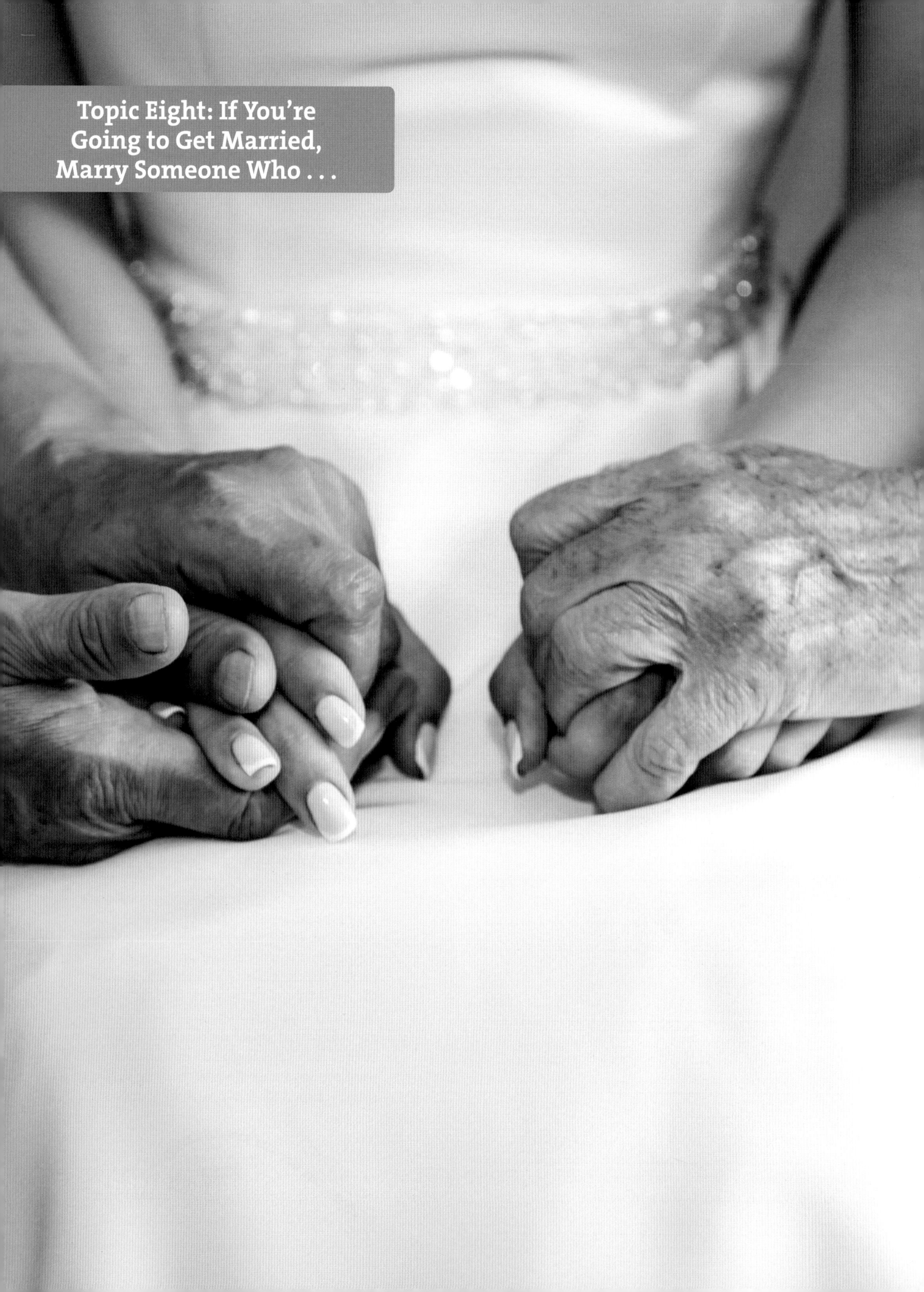

A Lutheran man married a Catholic woman. Neither was going to change religions for the other. They decided that any sons would be raised Lutheran, while daughters would be raised Catholic. The sons went to worship services with their dad. The daughters went to worship with their mother.

When it came to offerings, there were heated discussions. When the Lutheran church had a fund drive for something, the husband wanted to give extra. The husband could do that only if he gave the same extra amount to his wife's church. And when the wife's church asked for extra offerings, the wife would have to give the same amount to her husband's church. This caused some tense moments.

At home the parents taught their children that there was really no difference between Lutheran and Catholic. But when the children went to their respective religion classes, they learned that there were differences,

God has made some people who can live contented, upright lives without ever finding that "special someone." But what guidance can you give your grandchildren when they realize they weren't made to be single—when they are contemplating and dreaming about marriage?

Have you talked with your grandchildren about what to look for in a spouse?

There is something special about the relationship between grandparent and grandchildren. Many times, grandchildren will listen to and follow words of wisdom from a grandparent more than from parents. The words are coming from someone who has lived a longer life, enjoyed God's rich blessings, and endured good times and bad while being held on the lap of God's grace.

When it comes to marriage, some grandparents have big regrets: divorce, abuse, spiritual confusion in the home,

> "Whatever your marriage has been like, as Christian grandparents you have wisdom to share. Share it!"

which caused a lot of questions and, at times, more tense moments. The children were confused about religion and about whom to believe.

This is a true story. I was that husband's pastor for several years.

Not all marriages between people of different faiths are like that. Nor am I trying to say that marrying someone outside one's religion is some kind of sin. But sometimes when young people are busy falling head over heels in love, they don't think, "If we get married, will this person help me in my faith? help me raise our children to know the truth about Jesus?"

And, as important as those questions are, that's just the start. What are some other questions you would want your grandchildren asking as they evaluate a potential spouse? Does this person know what love really is, like in 1 Corinthians chapter 13? Does this person have the maturity to make a lifelong commitment? How does this person handle temptations like alcohol or pornography? What is this person's temper like?

etc. When your grandchildren are old enough to understand, be open with them about the lessons you have learned. Teach them what to watch out for, pray for, and look for in their future spouse.

Then again, many grandparents will have been married 30-40 years or longer. If your grandchild sees up close the loving, happy, Christ-centered marriage of their grandparents, they will take any of your advice to heart, because they want what Grandma and Grandpa have.

Remember, seeing your marriage will back up your words. Your example of how Christians live as husband and wife means so much. But don't just set the example. Talk about how it all happened.

Whatever your marriage has been like, as Christian grandparents you have wisdom to share. Share it!

Can you even broach the topic of "finding a spouse who will go to church with you"? Why not? An elderly grandma in my first congregation gave us a wall hanging that said, "The family that prays together, stays together."

To us that meant that we not only pray at home but also worship together as a family. By his grace, the Lord has been the center of our family life.

This is a real blessing.

The point is, God can use you, your prayers, and your guidance to help your grandchildren find spouses who will be great blessings to them, yes, and to their children!

Mentor Grandparents Respond

Su and Dave H. live in a small, rural midwestern resort community. Su is a cancer survivor (20 years!), and she maintains a supportive online ministry for others touched by cancer. They have grandchildren in Canada and Germany and treasure the times they are able to spend with family in person. Unfortunately, those moments are few and far between, so Su and Dave play the hand life has dealt them and find a way to make it work. They have embraced modern technology and have regular conversations with their grandkids via their computers and video chats.

They will be the first to say it is not ideal, but they will not let it stand in the way of building a relationship with their grandchildren. When Su recently let her 16-year-old grandson know that she and Dave had read an article about marriage and would like to talk with him about the topic, they could see his tense body language loud and clear across the miles. His immediate response was, "I don't know . . . I've got ten years or so!" A good laugh helped keep things light.

"I started him thinking by asking if he had any criteria, or what he might be looking for in a wife," Su explained. Their grandson did indeed have some (mostly domestic) ideas, making Su and Dave smile, enjoying their grandson's willingness to be open, even after being blindsided. "At this point," Su said, "Dave picked up on that and said, 'She would also be looking for some things that would be complementing *her*. How will you do *that* end of it?'"

Su said they also wanted to highlight marriages and anniversaries in their own family. Su's parents had been blessed with 70 years of marriage, and Su and Dave had just celebrated their 45th wedding anniversary. She wanted to stress that these things don't just happen.

They asked him, "What do you think of divorce?"

His response was, "I think it is like giving up on the other person." Su and Dave felt like this fit right in with everything they were trying to describe to him as the kind of marriage they were praying for him to be blessed with: prayerful, mutually respectful, selfless.

They were glad they had the conversation, and in the end it did not matter one bit that it relied on technology, versus waiting for a more ideal time to be in person. Despite the initial shock of Grandma and Grandpa throwing an unexpected topic at him, their grandson responded exceptionally well and even turned down an opportunity at one point to leave the conversation and go for a walk with friends. "He didn't act uncomfortable. He was open to listening," Su said.

Su described this combined article and conversation experience as a nudge to complete a mission that was already in her heart. "Those things were all thoughts that I had but had not made a point of sitting down and saying, but I will now with other grandchildren. It was something that was more important than I realized it would be."

~~~~~~~~~~

Sometimes the idea of staging a conversation about a major topic, like marriage, can be very intimidating for a grandparent. It doesn't have to be like that though, according to Carol V., an 86-year-old widow from Michigan. She has always lived near her grandchildren and played a part in their spiritual education, even teaching some of her own grandchildren in Sunday school.

After reading this article, Carol sat down with her 17-year-old granddaughter to have a conversation about marriage. She described what it was like to enjoy the years she had together with her husband before he passed away and the blessings she experienced in a Christian marriage. Then, not equating dating to marriage, but as an opportunity to let her granddaughter share her thoughts about the ways respectful relationships work, Carol turned the tables. "I asked her about her boyfriend, and she just started talking. She really opened up and talked a lot about the relationship. I was very happy. She was very grown up."

Carol is a gifted storyteller who can fill the time quickly with colorful anecdotes and lessons life has thrown her way. She also knows that there is a time to let others do the talking. This can be a challenging balance for grandparents who are very eager to share all the wisdom they have stored away. Sometimes it is difficult to ask an open-ended question and just sit back and listen to your grandchild's answer. But sometimes it is the best thing you can do.

~~~~~~~~~~

Jean K. experienced a very different scenario when she had a whole gaggle of grandchildren camping with her over the summer. She is an active 68-year-old widow with ten grandchildren ranging in age from 17 to 5.

While near the bonfire pit with two teenage brothers bantering about life, the topics of "Do you like some-one?" and "Do you have a girlfriend?" came up. Jean was able to squeeze in a few questions of her own: "Have you ever thought about the type of girl you'd want to marry? Have you thought about your parents' marriage? Is your parents' marriage different than the way they love you?"

The good-natured boys let Grandma right into their conversation. "Well, yeah," they both said. "That is the one person you share *everything* with. The good and the bad."

In a world where the word *love* seems to be overused and watered down, Jean said she was glad to see that the boys seemed to understand that in marriage, love is powerful and different and finds its strength rooted in the Bible. That was the answer she was listening for and was pleased to hear.

Notes

_____

_____

_____

_____

_____

_____

_____

Moving Forward

It is important that you and your grandchildren have a shared definition of Christian marriage. Anybody can go to a courthouse and seek a legal document to reflect that a marital contract has been entered into. Ask your grandchild why they think Christians go further. Look at these Bible passages together as you discuss God's intentions for establishing this holy union. Psalms 127 and 128 are good, as well as the duties of husbands and wives in the first half of 1 Peter chapter 3 or the second half of Ephesians chapter 5. Even some of the youngest children can be reminded where the strength to love comes from—Jesus' love for us at the cross: "We love because he first loved us" (1 John 4:19). More mature grandkids might be ready to tackle 1 Corinthians chapter 7 or the topic of divorce in Matthew chapter 19.

If there is a current boyfriend or girlfriend, show interest in hearing about them, like Carol did. Be careful not to tease or embarrass. "How did you meet?" "What are some of the favorite memories you have made together?"

Take advantage of opportunities God gives you to point out to your grandkids Christian marriages around you or around them that you see as healthy examples and talk about what makes you perceive them that way.

Topic Nine: God Keeps His Promises

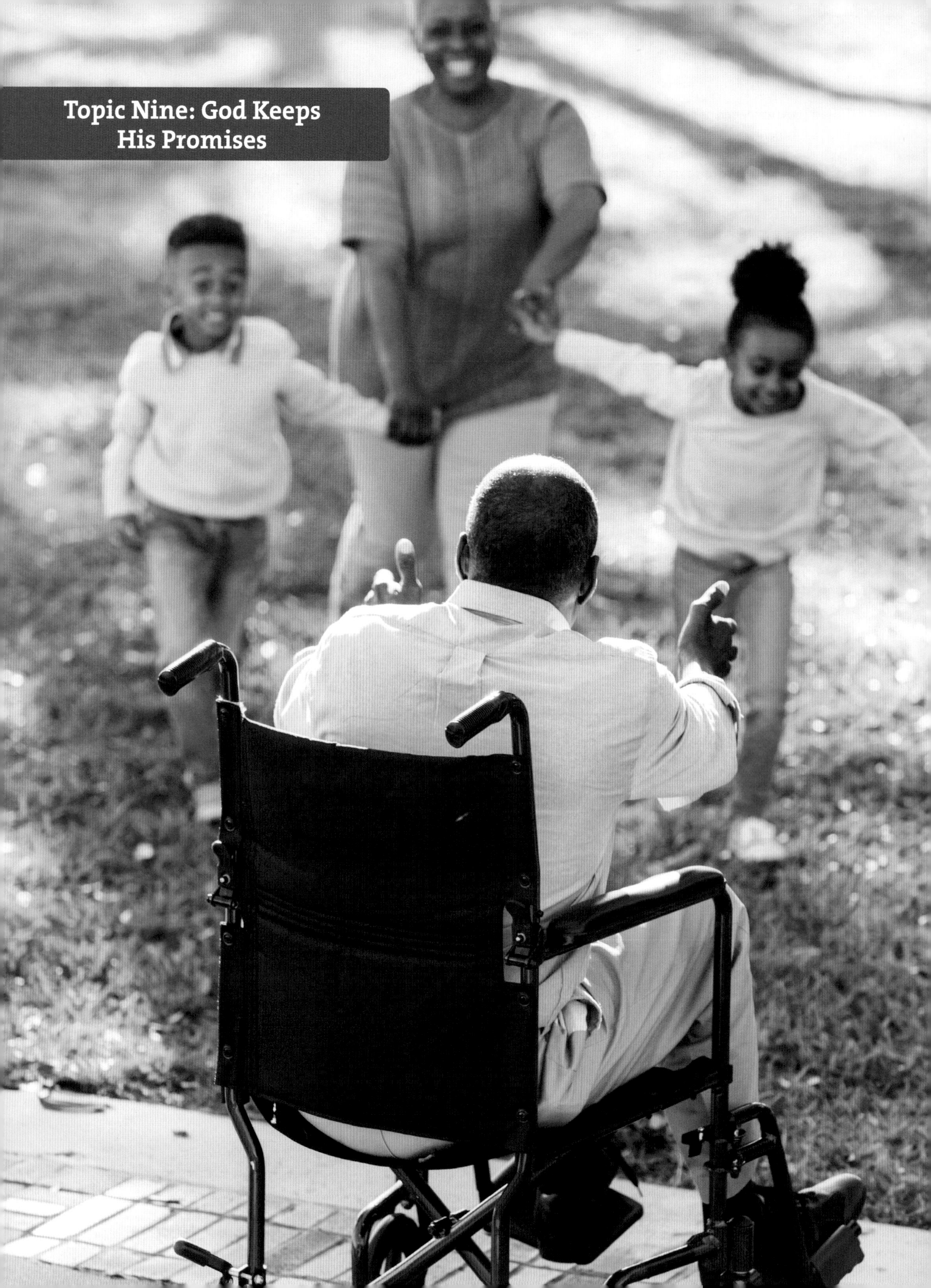

There are times when we struggle with doubts and fears, when the promises of God don't seem to apply to us. King David was in that kind of struggle when he wrote Psalm 13. Hear his frustration when he says, "How long must I wrestle with my thoughts and day after day have sorrow in my heart?" (Psalm 13:2). Our grandchildren need us to be honest like that with them about life. It won't do to gloss things over and pretend there are no concerns.

We also need to give them hope. Consider this all-purpose promise found in Romans 8:28: "We know that in all things God works for the good of those who love him."

Don't we know the truth of that from our own experience of seeing him keep his promises to us for the many decades of life he has given us? There was a time early in my ministry when this passage was of great help. I had to have jaw surgery. It required that I stay in the hospital for five days. There were many weeks after that of painful recovery.

all we can so those we love will keep trusting in God's promises. We don't want to put this off.

I wonder if you couldn't make a list right now of two or three times in your life when God kept his promise and surprised you by the way things worked out for your good. . . .

Do your grandchildren know those stories about you?

There are obstacles. It is easy to sing "Jesus loves me" with a child small enough to sit on your lap. It is more difficult as they get older to talk about God's promises. Teens tend to tighten up. They may be respectful and polite but keep their thoughts to themselves.

Maybe you could loosen them up a bit with a question. "What are some promises of God you've been thinking about lately?" or "Did I ever tell you about that time I was having doubts about one of God's promises?" or "Do you know about the time in my life when a promise of God surprised me?"

> ## Make a list right now of two or three times in your life when God kept his promise and surprised you.

This took time and energy away from my work as a pastor. Yet, reflecting on it later, I realized the experience actually helped my ministry. I could better relate to members I visited in the hospital. My devotional messages with them were enriched because of when I myself had needed to rely on God to pull me through.

Throughout my life I see my loving heavenly Father keeping this promise to work all things for my good. I see it in how he gave me a loving Christian wife and children and, yes, grandchildren. It is there in the way he has always provided for my needs and all sorts of luxuries beyond the actual needs. Above all, he gave his one and only Son to redeem me from my sins. There is such joy in looking forward to being in our heavenly home, thanks to Jesus.

These are things we want to communicate to our grandchildren, aren't they? Troubles will come and tempt our grandchildren into doubt: deaths, military deployments, a parent losing a job, not making the team, being bullied, etc. The world won't point them to God's promises—the world is spinning wildly away from the truths the Holy Spirit reveals in Scripture. We Christian grandparents need to be doing

Above all, let them know how important to you God's promise is about Jesus being our Savior from sin. Our goal is to bring them to the place King David got to when he concluded Psalm 13 with such joy and confidence: "I trust in your unfailing love; my heart rejoices in your salvation" (verse 5). Just as David in this psalm went from day after day of sorrow to the heights of joy, so can we all. Encourage your grandchildren whenever you can to trust in God's unfailing love. His plans for us are flawless. God always keeps his promises.

Dear Lord Jesus, help me to light the way for my grandchildren with the light you give us in your Word. Amen.

Mentor Grandparents Respond

Jeff D. is a grandfather of nine and lives along the rural Wisconsin-Minnesota border. You may remember him from a previous chapter, when we described the "Grandkid Camp" that he and his wife host each summer.

When Jeff read this article, he realized that while he had always shared funny stories of growing up to delight the grandchildren, there was a dark and serious side of his childhood that he had never opened up about. He had never described the reality of losing his father at such a young age, growing up with a single mother in a family with eight children. Jeff started thinking that it might be important for the grandchildren to learn that their happy, blessed grandpa grew up with both good and bad experiences. "There were a lot of things we went through as kids—that I personally went through as a kid—that you don't think about at the time . . . God is carrying you through." It is important to share the struggles too, he says, to teach them that "they need to turn to the Lord in all these things because he is in control. The challenges for my mom and the great appreciation I have for her . . . I see the Lord's hand. We were all loved. Mom had a magnificent load to bear, and the

Speaking to her nine-year-old grandson on the phone, she asked, "Can you tell me a little about some of God's promises?"

"Well," came the confident answer, "God always keeps his promises."

"Of course," she responded. "But can you tell me what some of them are?"

"Well, he promises to always love us. And he'll come back to earth to separate us from the unbelievers and decide if we're going to heaven or hell," he explained.

"And where do you think you'll be going?" she asked.

> "He gave his grandkids living proof that when bad things happen, God is always present to help us through."

Lord carried her through . . . and us. We always had warm beds, food to eat, our church family, neighbors, and other good people God sent."

"I had an opportunity when tucking kids in over Thanksgiving when the grandchildren were gathered at our house. It got late and we didn't have a big devotion. Instead, I took time in their rooms and I shared with them 'a great-grandpa they never met.' I told them that even though my family didn't have a dad, God put other people in our life who helped us grow up. The Lord took care of us."

While some people may think kids need to be sheltered from scary topics, what Jeff did is really important. He gave his grandkids a true gift of assurance by offering living proof that when bad things happen, God is always present to help us through. Jeff focused on the positives that came from a negative situation, and surely his grandchildren could see that they come from a family tradition where God's promises are taken very seriously.

⁓⁓⁓⁓⁓⁓⁓⁓⁓

Mishon Z. raised five children and is currently a 52-year-old grandmother with four grandkids. She always talked in a very matter-of-fact tone about spiritual topics with her own children as they were growing up, and it is no different with her grandchildren.

"Oh, I'll be in heaven—he said he made me a room. And another promise is that he's always with us, so we'll never have to be afraid."

Mishon wanted to include her six-year-old granddaughter too, so she asked him to pass the phone to his sister. Of course the little sister was ready to share her ideas as well, and they wisely included some Old Testament Bible stories, such as the great flood that was followed by a rainbow.

But the sweet, pint-sized evangelist was just getting started, because to Mishon's delight, she just kept rattling off more and more promises. "We never have to be scared, because he's always with us. We can't see him, but he's always with us. He always forgives us, even when we're naughty. He blesses us with good friends. Grandma . . . this is all I have in common with you!"

Mishon knew exactly what her granddaughter was trying to say, even though kindergartners don't quite have the most sophisticated use of language yet. "Well, we *do* have a lot in common, *don't* we!" she laughed.

_____

_____

_____

_____

_____

_____

_____

_____

_____

_____

_____

_____

_____

Moving Forward

Some grandkids may not even know what the phrase "God's promises" refers to. You might start with helping them to learn the Bible passages that are your favorite promises. Ask, "How can we be sure God will keep that promise and do what he says?"

(If you feel pretty unfamiliar with God's promises, you might start with Psalm 46:1, "God is our refuge and strength, an ever-present help in trouble," or Jesus' words in John 10:28 about how no one can snatch us out of his protecting hand. Or just Google "favorite Bible promises.")

When grandchildren are older, the promises that you "have in common" probably feel more serious. Just like this chapter's article suggests, it is important to talk to grandkids about times in _your_ life when you thought all was lost, but somehow circumstances changed and—just like God had promised—he pulled you through. In hindsight (or maybe you knew all along), it became clear that God turned your "hopeless" situation into something good. (Have you traced back through all the personal disasters of your life to see God's hand and the great care he displayed for you?) Ask your grandchildren if they have ever thought they were in situations over their head. Share stories that reflect God's unfailing love and God's long-term vision vs. our short sightedness.

Topic Ten: I Know I'm Going to Heaven

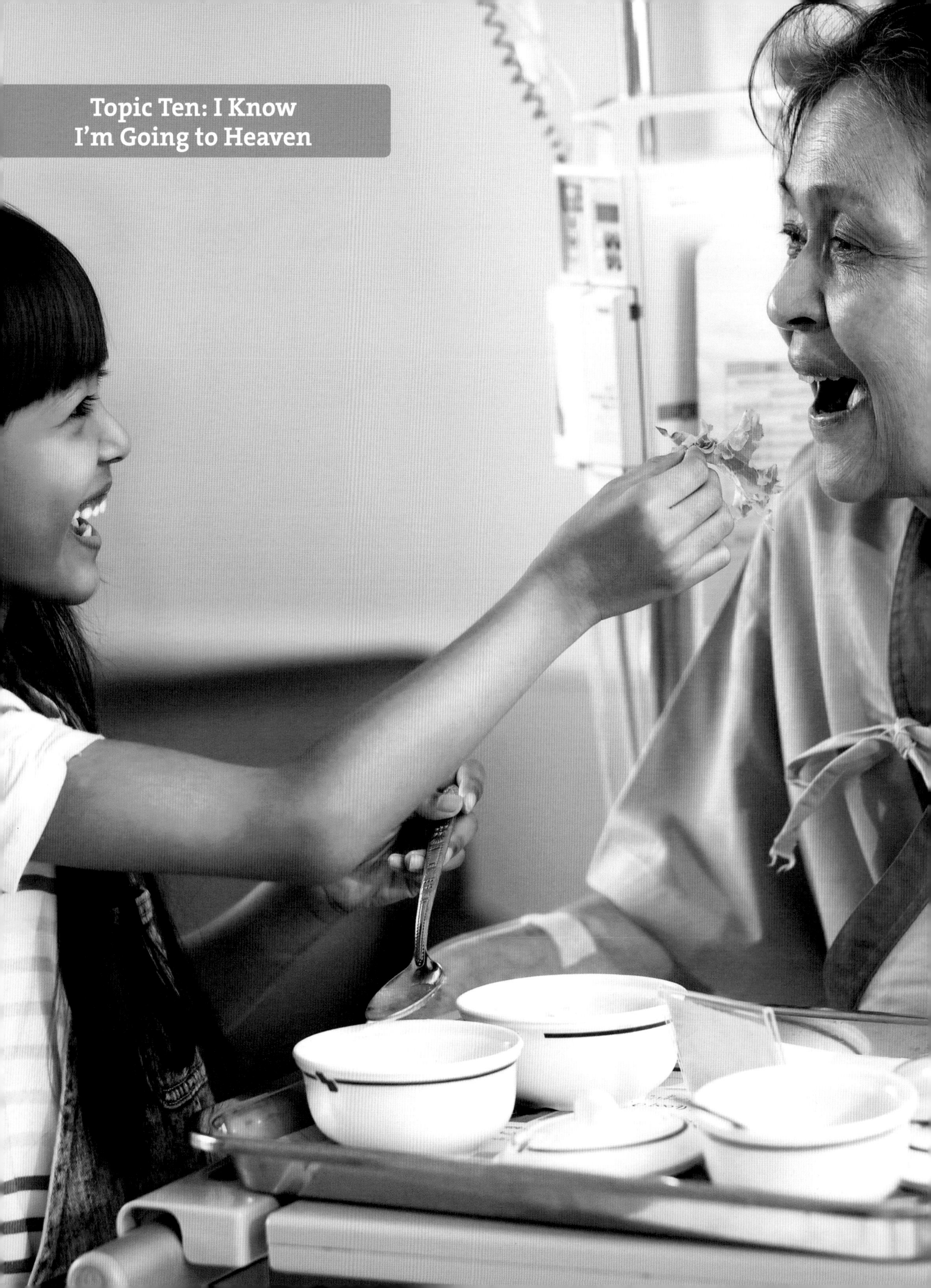

Grandma didn't think to tell me. She was too focused on dying. But I needed to know because there wasn't much time to be sure.

"Soon you will meet God. Are you ready?"

Now, my grandma was a collection of faiths. In the old country, she was Greek Orthodox. After coming to the United States as a young woman, she had tried Catholicism and Lutheranism, studied with the Jehovah's Witnesses and the Seventh-Day Adventists, and ended her life as a member of a community Baptist church.

"How can you be sure Grandma? Will God take you to heaven because you are so good?"

"No," she said, "I am not good."

She quickly said, "Yes," and then slowly shook her head no.

I said, "That's okay. Many people are confused about the way to heaven. Some think that they have to 'make their peace with God' before they die. This is an impossible thing for me to do. Grandpa does things wrong—he is sinful—and you have seen it. I can never make peace with God when every sin I do breaks the peace and makes war on God. So God made the peace between him and me. That's why he sent his Son, Jesus, into our world. I couldn't keep God's commandments no matter how hard I tried, but Jesus did! He did that for me! He is good, and God counts Jesus' goodness as mine. When Jesus died on the cross, he died for my sins—all my sins, every sin I have ever done. Jesus forgives me! Because of Jesus, there are no sins to keep me out of heaven. Jesus

"Her answer comforted me in the days to come. It gave me courage to hope as I sat by her coffin."

I was testing her. "Then it must be because you gave so much money to God. Surely that will buy you heaven."

"No, no one buys their way into heaven."

"Then why should God ever let you in?"

Her answer comforted me in the days to come. It gave me courage to hope as I sat by her coffin. It demonstrated to me how Christians live and die and live again: "Jesus died for me on the cross! He will give me heaven!"

I responded, "I will see you again. Jesus promises that too!"

We need to have this conversation with the grandchildren. The certainty of heaven is the only truth that calms the hearts of spectators to the dying process. In faith, we are sure that heaven will be ours one day. Use your certainty of eternal life to raise the sights of mourning grandkids and let the Holy Spirit work through your conversation to give another generation this same hope!

My eight-year-old granddaughter was sitting beside me in church. The pastor had done a wonderful job of laying out God's plan for our eternal rescue. I asked her, "Do you understand what Pastor said?"

will take my arm and walk me right through the front gate! I believe this. I'm certain of heaven because Jesus won it for me! God promises me this is true in his Word, and God has never lied to me or you in the Bible."

My granddaughter smiled at me and laid her head on my shoulder for the rest of the church service.

It is so important to talk to my grandkids about the saving love of Jesus that I have chosen to teach Sunday school. Picture it: white-haired old grandpa, sitting in front of 18 children—as many as five of them my grandchildren! We talk about the "true promises" God makes us in his powerful Word. We are amazed at every miracle our great God performs! But always we come back to the Lord's eternal love seen in the life, death, resurrection, and ascension of his one and only Son, Jesus! We follow Jesus through his life all the way to heaven and then celebrate together that we will be with him in heaven someday too!

The Holy Spirit has made you certain of eternal life in Christ. Trust the same Spirit to work the certainty of faith in other hearts. Teach them: "'Jesus loves me, this I know, for the Bible tells me so!' I am certain I'll be in heaven!"

Mentor Grandparents Respond

Laura R. is a 67-year-old grandmother, married for 45 years, who teaches at a day care. She also raised five children.

For the conversation about heaven, Laura knew that the grandchild she wanted to have a conversation with would be her ten-year-old granddaughter, so that is who she called. She talked to the parents first and then got to work.

The father of her granddaughter's friend had recently died, making this a very timely topic. It was a perfect opening to the conversation. "I'm going to talk to you about your friend. What is something sad that recently happened?" Laura asked.

"We shelter kids from death," Laura says. "We don't give kids enough credit. It's not a sad time."

Laura said the same words to her granddaughter. "It's not a sad time!"

To which her granddaughter responded, "Yeah! Because we're in heaven!"

~~~~~~~~~~

Carol, who also participated in the conversation about marriage, tried this conversation with her 13-year-old granddaughter. They spend a lot of time together, and she knows that her granddaughter will have a hard time someday when God calls Carol home.

"We shelter kids from death. We don't give kids enough credit."

"Her dad passed away," came the answer.

"You know someday I and Grandpa and others will pass away also and go to heaven," Laura continued.

"I know," she answered in a very comfortable tone. Laura was happy to hear that the conversation was pleasant and continued along the path by asking her granddaughter, "How do we know that I'll go to heaven and that Grandpa will go to heaven?"

With absolute confidence, her granddaughter answered, "Because when we were babies we were baptized."

For the remainder of their phone conversation, as Laura asked things like, "But how will I get to heaven?" every time her granddaughter gave her an answer, Laura kept asking her, "Why?" and her granddaughter kept on giving her Bible-based answer after answer. To say Laura was impressed is an understatement.

"I never expected her to start talking about Baptism! To me, that was special." While Laura might not necessarily rely on "Why?" as the main talking point for every conversation, in this particular moment it kept the momentum going and her granddaughter fed off of it.

"I've talked with her many times. She understands. She's very creative and sensitive. She understands exactly," Carol said.

Carol chose to sit down together in her home and talk about the Bible account of Jairus' daughter. In that lesson from the Bible, Jesus performed a miracle and brought a little girl back to life. He showed his almighty power over death. Carol talked about how she was certain that after her death, Jesus would give her eternal life in heaven. "The look on my granddaughter's face . . ." Carol trailed off. "This talk is just something that has to be done. You can help them in the long run if you talk about it now. You have to start somewhere."

Not all conversations with teens elicit wild response, and Carol remembers more of a good feeling from the talk rather than the specific words her granddaughter said back to her. Some conversations are like that, and they are still good conversations.

~~~~~~~~~~

Notes

Moving Forward

Your conversations about heaven might have to be different based on the ages of your grandchildren. When my young children first experienced seeing a deceased body at a funeral, they had questions about the person's soul. I compared it to a butterfly that had come out of a cocoon. The shell of the person we knew was left behind for us to see, but the actual "being" had gone to live with Jesus in heaven. Once again, be open to whichever direction the conversation takes, as you can't always control what happens to a topic once you bring it up.

If you have a chance to be together, you could show your grandchild where to find some of the beautiful resurrection passages in the Bible. John 11:25 is a treasured one, where Jesus said, "I am the resurrection and the life. The one who believes in me will live, even though they die." Tell your grandchild, "Jesus is talking about me right there."

Somewhere along the line I heard a pastor make the suggestion to write out a statement of faith and keep it with your will and other legal documents for descendants to find after you are gone. After reading this article, I can't help but think what a gift of peace this would be for a grieving family. Anyone at any age can write a statement of faith and save it inside their Bible or someplace special. Why not spend some time writing together with your grandchild?

Conclusion

Linda T. is a retired teacher from Minnesota who has four grandchildren. Two of them live near Linda and her husband, Dick. The other two grandchildren live in Colorado, where Dick and Linda schedule an annual trip that lasts a minimum of six weeks, in order to provide a chance to adequately catch up. Linda has some great advice to share based on conversations she had while teaching and substituting in lower and middle grade classrooms.

"Some of the best discussions we had were not a part of the plan or the curriculum but were based on what the kids said," Linda observed. This backs up the idea mentioned several times, that it is alright when conversations don't go exactly according to plan. In fact, you might end up with something even better than you could have hoped for, if you are willing to let the grandchild take the lead (and the Holy Spirit, who guides our efforts to talk about his Word).

Linda also said, "I think sometimes kids think about things a lot before they actually say it. They have to get bold enough to say it. They maybe hint at something, but then you have to set things aside and dig deeper. Take the moment when it happens."

As much as possible, Linda encourages being accessible to your grandchildren so they will be comfortable turning to you for important conversations and you will grow to become perceptive to their communication methods. In her situation, she admits that she and her husband have to work really hard at making sure they are bonding with the out-of-state grandchildren the same as the closer ones. They do schedule a long stay with the Colorado grandchildren each year, but during the other months they heavily depend on the phone, e-mail, and Skype for building their relationships. She says, "You've gotta grab the moment, but to grab the moment, you've gotta be there to listen!"

When Linda thought about her place in this world as a grandparent and the challenges today's generation faces, she said, "The forces of evil are strong, but God is stronger. It makes a grandparent's role more important. Grandparents have a lot more responsibility, as part of the extended family . . . there is a generational job . . . a family calling of holding the family together."

~~~~~~~~~~

Carol from Michigan, our oldest grandmother at 86, had some similar thoughts that seem important yet to share. "You have to keep trying. You can't think about yourself. You have a job to do as a parent or a grandparent, and talking isn't going to hurt anyone. Their future is important. When you have a child, you have a responsibility so they can live in eternity."

The beauty of all the attempted conversations during (what I called) The Grandparent Project is that there seems to be literally no way a conversation could fail. In the best of situations, the grandchild responded perfectly on cue and the conversation happened without a hitch. In the worst of situations, the experience was like using an under-used muscle in your body: awkward, perhaps, but nobody was harmed and it ended up being excellent groundwork for the next attempt.

By the time you talk your way through the topics suggested in this book, you'll be experts at discussing all the most important topics of the day. I pray that you continue your spiritual conversations as well, perhaps using your pastor's weekly sermon topic as an easy one to start with. As your grandchildren grow up, maybe you pick a devotion book to work through together and share notes. I am confident that our God will continue to bless you with every opportunity to "tell the next generation the praiseworthy deeds of the LORD, his power, and the wonders he has done" (Psalm 78:4).

THINGS to Tell Your Grandkids